CAPE COD WILDFLOWERS

CAPE COD WILDFLOWERS

A Vanishing Heritage

Mario J. DiGregorio
Jeff Wallner

University Press of New England
Hanover and London

Published by University Press of New England
37 Lafayette Street
Lebanon, NH 03766

Originally published as *A Vanishing Heritage: Wildflowers of Cape Cod* in 1989 by Mountain Press Publishing Company, Missoula, MT. Reissued by arrangement with Mountain Press Publishing Company.

ISBN 1–58465–319–1

Printed in China 5 4 3 2 1

CIP data appear on the last page of the book

Acknowledgements

The authors wish to acknowledge the people who encouraged us to produce this updated edition of *A Vanishing Heritage*. It is our hope that this book still reminds Cape Codders that the fate of our botanic treasures are as fragile today as they were in 1989, the date of our original publication.

To Beth Schwarzman, author of *The Nature of Cape Cod* (University Press of New England, 2002), who directed the authors to seek a new publication edition with UPNE; to our fellow field botanists; Pamela Polloni, Ann Buckley, Donald Schall, Nancy Wigley, Dr. Richard Backus, Dr. Richard and Teresa Norris, Dr. Paul Cavanagh, Karen Wilson, Anne Wagner, Dr. Aimlee Laderman, and Dr. Paul Somers, Program Botanist for the Division of Fisheries and Wildlife's Natural Heritage and Endangered Species Program. Thanks to all for providing technical expertise and the most valuable of commodities, camaraderie in the field.

We wish to extend special gratitude to our editors at University Press of New England; M. Ellen Wicklum, Richard Pult, Production Assistant Douglas C. Tifft and UPNE Director Richard Abel.

Contents

Preface to the New Edition
Cape Cod 2003

"It is a Wild rank place, and there is no flattery in it"
— Henry D. Thoreau, 1857

PADDLING UP THE MASHPEE RIVER on a recent warm summer day, we were moved by the wonderful palette of color from the riverbank: the brilliant scarlet of cardinal flowers, lavender hue of climbing boneset, pink turtle head and sky-blue of forget-me-nots. Together, these may be but a mere relic of a time long past when Cape Cod was indeed a "wild, rank place." The Mashpee River Park protects the shoreline, marsh and upland bluffs overlooking one of the last great tidal freshwater rivers remaining on Cape Cod. President Grover Cleveland fished and hunted here; Wampanoag regard it as a center of spiritual power (along with the nearby Noisy Hole wetland); it has not quite been discovered by modern tourism.

Land planning visionaries and land trusts have attempted to link large open space acquisitions to create contiguous wildlife corridors for migration, shelter and re-colonizing. Creative acquisition strategies often involve a quiltwork of private, state, federal and municipal open space in stitching together these "emerald necklaces." This creates a real functioning habitat and not a cookie-cutter network of small, checkerboard enclaves. The Mashpee River National Wildlife Refuge is a prime example of this cooperative approach to land acquisition and habitat protection.

Since the original publication of *A Vanishing Heritage* in 1989, two significant events have slowed the development and accelerated the protection of significant open space in Barnstable County: the creation of the Cape Cod Commission, and the passage of the First Barnstable County Land Bank Bill.

The Cape Cod Commission is a countywide policy and regulatory review agency. The commission's jurisdiction is over the largest, most potentially damaging projects. It works through the Development of Regional Impact (DRI) review process. The lines are drawn and the debate is at times a rancorous one between the forces of development and those of preservation. Memories of the wholesale plunder of the Cape and Islands landscape in the mid to late 1980s by overzealous developers leaves little choice to beleaguered Cape Codders. We should unstintingly support this vitally important watchdog regulatory agency.

The Land Bank Bill was watered down considerably in the political process. The remaining legislation provides important funding procured via a self-imposed twenty-year tax on real estate. Cape Cod landowners in each of the county's fifteen towns pay this surcharge to fund open space land purchases. While this has hardly been a panacea in the aggressive and expensive Cape real estate market, it is at least a step forward in protection of the last undeveloped land in Barnstable County.

In 2001, the U.S. Census Bureau projected an increase of 19 percent in the year-round population of Cape Cod from 1980 figures. This means an estimated change from 185,000 to 220,000. Given that the latter figure may nearly triple by the summer season of 2010, the transportation infrastructure of the Cape (i.e. bridges, Mid-Cape Highway, rotaries and connector roads) will by then be woefully inadequate.

So what does this all mean for our wildflowers?

Every new development, from a commercial strip mall to a fifty-lot residential subdivision, brings with it short-term consumptive "progress." Long-term impacts include: ever-expanding lawns, domestic pet predation, and the depletion of our natural resources for so-called "recreational" pursuits. At risk: our peninsula's fragile sandplain grasslands, coastal kettle ponds, barrier beaches and heathlands.

Let's look at two recent examples of the developmental impacts to our native flora. In 1998, purple milkweed (*Asclepias purpurascens*) was discovered growing within one hundred feet of a new gas station/strip mall in Hatchville. There has been no other recent documentation of this flower elsewhere in Massachusetts. The three milkweed plants, hanging by the thread of existence, were browsed to the ground by hungry deer in 2001. Currently, the milkweed site is threatened to become a patio-lawn store. It remains to be seen if this attractive and rare wildflower will survive the vicissitudes of man and deer in the coming season.

The "Green Death" is another example. Every road improvement brings with it something I call "The Green Death." This emerald-shaded slurry is technically known as hydro seeding. Hydro seeding involves a green-dyed mush sprayed over newly installed water and gas lines. The result is a mix of alien and naturalized grasses and "meadow in a can" frauds. The species used in this process are not generally indigenous to our maritime region. Its victims include the yellow thistle (*Cirsium horridulum*, page 74). This inconspicuous and overlooked roadside beauty once grew for many years in our neighborhood. After a recent road widening and repaving job, these curious sandplain flowers have vanished beneath the green slime. Who will notice their demise?

The wonder and serenity of the natural world is a vital part of our existence. Yet, despite our troubled and uncertain times, the spring flowering season brings with it promise, hope, and true reliability. The spring's first mayflower and bird-foot violet means more to us now than ever before. Let's not allow progress to wreak havoc on our natural heritage.

— mjd

A Heritage of Wildflowers

IN THE MID-1800's Harvard botanist Asa Gray produced a series of impressive botanical texts which helped to popularize the study of wildflowers. His 1887 *School and Field Botany* introduced a generation of students to the intricacies of flower structure and species identification. The fine points of the science, then and now, included understanding terms such as "hirsute","herborization", and "loculicidal dehiscence".

Gray called his text "a companion and interpreter....by which the student threads his flowery way to a clear knowledge of the vegetable creation." From our late twentieth century vantage point, the idea of botany in the public schools is quaint, at best. But the generation Gray helped to produce was one keenly aware of natural history. It was the generation that gave us the first National Parks, the Audubon Societies, the Conservation movement.

American explorers, poets, and leaders had long been drawn to botany. Lewis and Clark brought back hundreds of plant specimens for Thomas Jefferson. The Transcendentalists, Emerson, Thoreau, and others, made the study of the natural world a kind of ritual. Walt Whitman recovered from a paralyzing stroke by studying flowers along a New Jersey creek. Man-of-action John Muir decorated his journals with tender renditions of Sierra wildflowers. Theodore Roosevelt wrote narratives of native vegetation he found in Africa and on the Amazon River.

But the botanical fervor of the late nineteenth century was not confined to the artistic and political leadership. Everyone it seemed, was looking at, identifying, or collecting flowers. The New York businessman scanning the pages of *The Journal of Commerce*, a predecessor of the Wall Street Journal, would be able to read, on page one, an updated list of the wildflowers currently in bloom in New Hampshire's White Mountains. The summer people who took the air in New England resorts were hooked on a new outdoor sport: botanizing.

Cape Cod's summer set went along with the fashion. The fine record we have of the historical distribution and abundance of wildflowers on the Cape is partly due to their work. These amateurs added to professional herbaria of Harvard and the New England Wildflower Society samples of the latest discoveries from the edge of a Cape Cod pond or the back of a Nantucket dune. To this day, scholars sift through the records and specimans of that era, seeking clues to the whereabouts of our rarest plants.

From a modern vantage, it is easy to scoff at the old-fashioned wildflower enthusiasts. In the light of our high-tech recreational activities, their simple pursuits seem simple-minded. Do we really want to go back to those times? Go back to a naivete that believed all orchids were made for plucking? No. Back to a knowledgeable and appreciative public, willing and able to rise to the defense of native plants? Absolutely.

We share Cape Cod with a spectacular variety of natural species. Our native plants are dependent on the sand and gravel soils left behind by Ice Age glaciers. We enjoy the company of many southern species found no where else in New England, thanks to a climate moderated by the ever-present ocean. Our natural heritage includes a pleasing mix of habitats, from wooded hollows to windy sand plains, from tidal mud flats to sandy beaches, each with its own community of wildflowers.

But the floral richness of Cape Cod has a human side as well. From Wampanoag healers to Mayflower settlers, from cottage gardeners to modern developers, we've all had a stake in the fate of our wildflowers.

This book is an appreciation, a guide, and a plea for protection. On one hand it explores the arcane lore of the medieval herbalists, the classic derivation of plant names, the antique charm of colonial household uses. On the other, it chronicles the latest scientific understanding of flowers' ecological importance and current attempts to preserve natural diversity.

Those who work and play in this rapidly developing region must be made aware of the loss of habitat that threatens our wildflowers. Modern Cape Codders, vistors or residents, need to renew aquaintance with the colors that brighten our world. What follows is only an invitation to exploration; an attempt to turn the gaze of the Cape's bustling population back to this quiet,unassuming, heritage of flowers.

Using This Book

A Vanishing Heritage is arranged in chapters based on habitat types. All flowers have preferred soils and climates in which they grow best. Some cross borders and inhabit several different environments. More than other flowers,our rare and endangered species are confined to very specific habitats.

If you are using this book for quick field identification, be aware of its limited scope. Many of our showiest native flowers can be found here by simply flipping through the book. But most common roadside weeds and garden escapees have not been included. In fact, this book contains but 66 of the 1300 species of vascular plants found on the Cape. We hope that this appreciation and introduction to the most prized of Cape wildflowers will lead the reader to broader field guides and then to the botanical texts needed to identify our rarest flowers.

Each entry is made directly opposite a full color picture of the flower. One or more common names are given, followed by a scientific name of Greek or Latin origin. The scientific name consists of the *genus* name, shared by closely related plants, and the specific or *species* name of that particular kind. The scientific name is followed by an abbreviation which identifies the scientist who first named the plant. Some species have additional names denoting varieties and subspecies which differ in small detail from the species as originally described. Scientific nomenclature follows the *Manual of Vascular Plants of Northeastern United States and Adjacent Canada*, 2nd ed. (Henry A. Gleason & Arthur Cronquist; N.Y. Botanical Garden, 1991).

The text explores the lore of the plant in both natural and human history and describes threats to its existence. Interesting derivations of plant names are explored, and descriptions of peculiar features of the plant are given. At the end of each entry the reader will find dates that indicate when the flower will be found in bloom, and hints as to the best places to seek the plant.

The photographs were virtually all taken at wild stations of the plants within the region by the senior author using a Canon AT-1 camera, with both macro and conventional lenses and Kodak Ektachrome film. Authorship of each chapter is denoted by initials after the habitat introduction.

Attributions: The abbreviation which appears after the scientific names of each wildflower in this book give credit to the botanist who first discovered and named the species. Listed here are the names of these pioneers:

L. - Carolus Linnaeus

Ait. - William Aiton

Bess. - Wilibald Swibert Josef Gottlieb Besser

Bickn. - Eugene Pintard Bicknell

Bigel. - Jacob Bigelow

DC. - Augustin Pyramus DeCandolle

Fern. - Merritt L. Fernald

Hook. - William Jackson Hooker

Lam. - Jean Baptiste Pierre Antoine de Monet de Lamarck

Marsh. - Humphrey Marshall

Michx. - Andre Michaux

Nutt. - Thomas Nuttall

Raf. - Costantine Samuel Rafinesque-Scmaltz

R. Br. - Robert Brown

Sw. - Olaf Swartz

Thunb. - Carl Pehr Thunberg

Torr. - John Torrey

Willd. - Karl Ludwig Willdenow

The Area Covered By This Book

There are geographical, political, sociological, and commercial definitions of just where Cape Cod begins.

A Vanishing Heritage features wildflowers found in the southern half of Plymouth County and all of Barnstable County, Massachusetts. Although politically separate, and physically divided by the man-made Cape Cod Canal, these areas have a common natural and human heritage. Geologically they share Ice Age origins as outwash plains or higher terminal moraines. Their ecological affinities are those of the northern coastal plain; the pond-edge flora of the mid-Cape can also be found around the inland ponds of Carver and Lakeville. The entire area enjoys an intimate relationship to the Atlantic Ocean and its moderate climate. There is shoreline on Cape Cod Bay and Buzzards Bay in both counties. Finally, the popular conception of their human heritage includes Wampanoag Indians, Pilgrim settlers, salty seafarers, and summer resorts.

We leave it to the our readers to decide where their own Cape Cod experience begins.

— jw

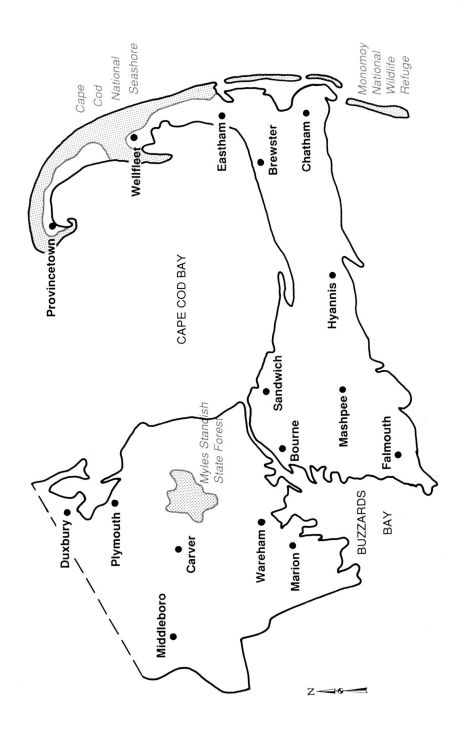

The area covered in this book

Woodlands

CAPE COD IS SO DOMINATED by the sand beaches of ocean and lake shores that its forests are easily overlooked. Yet, an aerial view reveals deep green vegetation covering most of the area. Visitors to the Cape drive along the densely wooded moraine ridge where the Mid-Cape highway runs, and they explore swamp forests on boardwalk trails in the Cape Cod National Seashore. Large patches of state-owned land — the Myles Standish Forest in Plymouth and Otis Air Base on the Cape — retain unbroken expanses of the original pine and oak forest cover.

When the Pilgrims reached the shores of Massachusetts Bay they sent back glowing reports about the forests. Seafaring peoples were interested in pine pitch, oak boards, and tall mast trees. One report from the New World waxed lyrical about the "juniper, birch, holly, vines, some ash, and walnut; wood for the most part open and without underwood." Today's tangles of greenbriar and scrub oak seem to contradict this glowing description. Historians have suggested that reports of 'forests you could ride through for miles' were propaganda efforts to convince the would-be colonist that America was not an impenetrable jungle!

The truth of the historical matter may never be settled, but the fact remains that after 350 years of white settlement the Cape's forest bears little resemblance to that known by the native Wampanoag bands. The original Cape Cod forests have suffered the ravages of storm, fire, erosion, tillage, lumbering, and strip-clearing for charcoal (to fire iron furnaces and saltworks). Neglect after burning and clearing led to the destruction of top soil and the creation of an oak-pine monoculture where once there was diversity.

3

Pitch pine and black oak are the dominant forest trees on the glacial outwash plains that dominate lower Plymouth County and the central ridges of Cape Cod. These trees are highly tolerant of drouthy soil where water quickly percolates down to the water table. Add to this the acidic conditions caused by decomposition of fallen leaves and needles and the forest becomes self-perpetuating. A dry understory of heaths — plants tolerant of acidity and nutrient deficiency — includes huckleberry, low blueberry, lambkill, and wintergreen.

Richer woodlands line the uplands around the shores of Cape Cod and Buzzards Bay. Here lake and ice edge deposits of glacial times left a substrate of water-holding materials. Pockets of hardwood growth can even be found in the scrub barrens of the Outer Cape where kettle holes penetrate the water table. Where not filled with lakes, these glacier-carved depressions may be home to Atlantic white cedar or red maple swamps, each with their own characteristic wildflowers.

With the exception of swamps, covered by wetland protection laws, there is little to stop development of our forests. The blanket of green covering Cape Cod has been divided into a crazy-quilt of house lots. We're fortunate that large acreages of forest are protected in state and national parks and by local conservation groups. But there are still rare plants, such as the mid-Cape's post oak, which rely on the sensitivity of thousands of individual landowners who now have a piece of our forest heritage in their backyards.

— jw

4

Trailing Arbutus or Mayflower

Jack-in-the-pulpit

Wintergreen, Checkerberry, or Teaberry

Swamp Honeysuckle

Pink Lady's-slipper or Moccasinflower

Trout Lily

Skunk Cabbage

Indian Pipes

Columbine

Lambkill or Sheep Laurel

Trailing Arbutus or Mayflower   *Epigea repens* L.

No wildflower, however showy or fragrant, is more eagerly awaited than the spring's first mayflower. Peeking out from the dried oak leaves of the forest floor, the pinkish blossoms of this ground-hugging plant banish for another year the dreary monotones of winter. Indeed, legend has it that the Pilgrims, despairing after that first terrible winter of 1620-21, were given new hope by the sight of these lovely flowers. (Trivia buffs should remember that the *Mayflower* which landed at Plymouth Rock was named after a European flower, the blossom of a crab apple tree.)

The dry sandy woods all along the Cape's high backbone are prime habitat for the trailing arbutus. Some south-facing road-cuts and banks are literally carpeted with the plant and the April sun raises a sweet scent from the newly opened flowers that's known to induce spring fever. *Epigea repens*, mayflower's Greek scientific name, means "crawling upon the earth," not exactly poetic but an apt description of the plant's growth habit. A walker may have to search a bit beneath last year's litter, but the discovery of a garland of mayflowers in full bloom is certainly worth the effort.

Mayflower sports oval, evergreen leaves and waxy five-petaled flowers. Its fragrance is described as spicy-sweet and the flowers taste as good as they smell. So attractive is this member of the Heath Family that it was once over-collected to the point of rarity. Today the plant is not as uncommon as it once was, though its appearance on the cover of National Wildlife's recent report on endangered species is a warning to us of its precarious position. Sad to say, roadside stands selling trailing arbutus can still be found in southeastern Massachusetts. The official state flower is a poor transplant and should be left in the wild to perfume the spring woodlands.

March - May   Sandy Woodlands

6

Trailing Arbutus or Mayflower *Epigaea repens*

Jack-in-the-pulpit   *Arisaema triphyllum* (L.) Schott

Gnomes of the plant world, the members of the Arum Family are bizarre denizens of wet woods, mostly tropical rain forests. Our swamps and damp woods harbor the Jack-in-the-pulpit with its three-leaved stalk sheltering a flowering spadix ("Jack") surrounded by a striped hood called a spathe ("the pulpit".) Common enough before extensive drainage and alteration of wetlands and watercourses, the Jack's sermon must now be searched out in forgotten wetlands.

The plant is sometimes called Indian turnip for the enlarged taproot or corm which is a problematical edible. These roots contain calcium oxalate crystals which are microscopic and knife-edged — giving new meaning to the phrase 'a sharp taste.' Most people experience a harsh burning reaction to raw Indian Turnip, but it is said that boiling or drying counters the effects of the crystals and produces a passable vegetable dish. (Remember though that when there were enough Indian turnips to satisfy native hunger, there weren't two convenience stores per mile along our Cape backroads.)

The sex life of the Jack-in-the-pulpit has been the subject of much discussion recently. Some plants are known to harbor both male and female flowers on the spadix, clustered in separate groups, male above and female below. Other, contrary, individuals abort all flowers of one gender during their early years and function as single-sexed (or dioecious) plants for a time. That is strange enough, but new research reveals that these plants make a mid-life correction and function as the other sex for the rest of their reproductive careers, thus getting the best of both worlds as Jacks *and* Jills in-the-pulpit.

May   Wet Woods, Swamps

8

Jack-in-the-pulpit *Arisaema triphyllum*

Wintergreen, Checkerberry, or Teaberry
Gaultheria procumbens L.

Years ago everyone was humming the catchy little "Teabery Shuffle" jingle. Gums, candies, medicines and various spirits are all flavored with oil of wintergreen — the essence of which is derived from the sweet birch tree. Chewing on birch bark is an interesting but not particularly gratifying pursuit. Fortunately for naturalists, a common Heath Family plant has concocted the very same flavor. Its shiny leaves and red berries (technically, overgrown 'capsules') are easy to find and when chewed they provide a natural breath freshener which is especially useful if your company in the woods is an interesting member of the opposite sex.

This plant has been called wintergreen, teaberry, checkerberry, boxberry, mountain tea and ivory-leaf. This proliferation of aliases should be taken as a sign not of notoriety, but of popularity. Invariably, when you have determined the plant's identity and proudly proclaim "That's wintergreen!" some wiser companion will say "My mother always called that checkerberry!" In such cases it may be advisable to memorize the scientific name and its meaning to dazzle the opposition. However, are you likely to remember that *Gaultheria* derives from Jean-Francois Gaultier (1708-1756), court physician at Quebec?

Call it what you will, the plant bears close inspection. Although its flowers are inconspicuous white bells, the shiny evergreen leaves catch the eye at all seasons. The red berries are more attractive than the flowers and since they persist through the winter months can be picked sparingly for a garnish to holiday dishes. When you pick a sprig of wintergreen you are taking but one branch from an unusual shrub. A procumbent look at *G. procumbens* will reveal that the stem sprawls along the ground. Thus, what looks like a colony of individuals, may be one, large multi-branched plant. Taken together, these attributes make wintergreen a popular nursery ground cover.

May - July   Dry woodlands

Wintergreen, Checkerberry, or Teaberry

Swamp Honeysuckle   *Rhododendron viscosum* (L.) Torr.

Nondescript, run-of-the-thicket shrubs standing in damp places seldom catch the eye. Yet, suddenly, in late June the swamp honeysuckle blares out clusters of white, trumpet-shaped flowers and has its time in the limelight. Honeysuckle is one of botany's most overused names, applied to many species of flowers whose resemblance goes no further than their fragrance — an indication that those who named them looked no further than their noses.

This sweet-scented shrub is a wild relative of our backyard rhododendrons and azaleas — a pure native strain thought superior by wildflower connoiseurs concerned with good breeding. Rhododendron species are mostly northern or mountain plants and are highly intolerant of limey soils. In fact, like all members of the Heath Family, they've special adaptations to sterile soils and do well in the sands of Plymouth County and the Cape.

Rhododendron is Greek for "rose-tree," a reference to the long cultivation of these showy shrubs. Gardeners point out that "the fancy varieties are much confused as to species." Red and carmine varieties of the swamp honeysuckle could also be confused with the more northerly pink azalea or the much rarer pinxter-flower which blooms before its leaves appear. Our swamp or "clammy" azalea is peculiar in having reddish hairs at the base of its flower tube — hairs that exude a sticky substance. Whether this substance attracts pollinators or repels unwanted predators is not entirely clear, but the adaptation serves as an easy mark of a plant which is hard to ignore at the height of its blooming season.

June-July   Wet woods, thickets, swamps

12

Swamp Honeysuckle   *Rhododendron viscosum*

Pink Lady's-slipper or Moccasinflower
Cypripedium acaule Ait.

Of the 20-odd species of orchids thought to occur on Cape Cod, the Lady's-slipper is easily the showiest and most common. Throughout its large range in the eastern United States this has proven to be the hardiest and most adaptable of its family. Also called Nerve-root, the flower has survived the depredations of herbalists seeking to make a sedative from its fibrous rhizomes, and misguided picking and transplanting by wildflower enthusiasts. Found on dry soils or in bogs, on coastal plains and mountainsides, the lady's-slipper is widely known and admired. A widespread belief that the flower is protected by law has helped it thrive, but as more and more of our upland woods become backyards, this orchid is faced with its most serious threat.

People are charmed by orchids — they remind us of tropical jungles where bizarre plants climb over each other in competition for light and nutrients. The peculiar structure and delicate color of the moccasinflower explains *our* fascination, but we ought to remember that the orchid flower was designed for the edification of insects. From a bee's eye view the lady's-slipper is irresistable. Sepals and petals, those portions of flowers usually responsible for attracting insects, are of little importance in orchids with one exception. The middle of its three petals has been modified by evolution into a large, inflated sac which is cleft down the middle — the 'slipper' of its name.

Drawn by the promise of a sugar "high" from the nectar inside, insects enter through the slit, which proves to be a one-way street. At first this may appear a trap, but even the most bumbling of bees eventually finds the exit. On the way out the insect is plastered with a natural glue on which, in turn, pollen is dusted. Emerging from the flower with cargo (of pollen) and payment (in nectar) the insect goes to another flower where, in the same intricate exit process, some of the pollen is deposited on the stigma to fertilize the plant and produce new seed.

The adaptations of orchids for insuring pollination are among nature's most elegant examples of evolution in action. The great number of orchid species world-wide are proof that new species are constantly evolving and were subjects of Darwin's research. Of all our orchids, the moccasinflower appears to be the most successful in this evolutionary game of trial and error.

May - June   Woods

Pink Lady's-slipper *Cypripedium acaule*

Trout Lily   *Erythronium americanum*   Ker Gawler

In consideration of those who know this flower by another name, we list the following synonyms: yellow adder's tongue, fawn lily, dogtooth violet. All of the flower's titles are descriptive. Trout and fawn lily refer to the spotted leaves which help to identify the plant even when not in bloom. (Trout and fawn skins, though little resembling each other, both bear spots.) Yellow adder's tongue seems to refer to the exerted reproductive organs of the flower — its 6 swept-back yellow tepals (a name referring to similarly colored petals and sepals) reveal a cluster of style and anthers that looks like the tongue of a snake.

But what of dogtooth violet and *Erythronium* which is Greek for 'red flower'? These names are carry-overs from a European species which is indeed violet-red and has short tuberous roots that resemble a canine tooth. Our flowers have the roots, but lack the violet color. Recently, scientists have decided that the former species name *americanum* which seemed appropriate enough for a represntative eastern woodland plant, must be replaced by *umbilicatum*, an obscure reference to the plant's structure.

A trout lily by any other name is still a delight of the Spring woods. One must often brave soggy ground to find these diminutive lilies, blooming long before leaves appear on the trees overhead. Belonging to a group of unrelated plants known as "Spring ephemerals", the fawn lily uses April sunshine to maximum advantage, spreading its shiny, energy-absorbing leaves broadside to the sun's rays. The flowers rise quickly, opening only when the sun is shining, not to waste pollen to storm winds or insect-less days. By the time the leaves emerge the plants have disappeared and by full summer all adder's tongues are dormant as underground tubers, waiting for next year's thaw to trigger another round of fast living.

April - May   Rich Woods

Trout Lily   *Erythronium americanum*

Skunk Cabbage   *Symplocarpus foetidus* (L.) Nutt.

A time-tested rite of spring in Massachusetts is to haunt some wet, greenbrier-guarded swamp, kneeling in the mud and sticking probing fingers into the weird, hood-like spathe of the skunk cabbage. A smile of triumph greets the sight of pollen grain stuck to the finger — sure signal that the first flowering has begun. Surprisingly enough, in some swamps near the coast of Buzzards Bay this event may take place in January!

Skunk cabbage has several adaptations which help it in this precocious flowering. First of all, as in most plants, this year's flowers actually budded last fall. But unlike other buds which remain unformed and hidden from the cold, the pointed spathes of skunk cabbage actually poke up out of their beds of wet moss in November and December. Then the metabolic process of cellular respiration produces enough heat to actually melt the snow around the emergent flower — creating a micro-oasis of warmth. Even the swamp habitat assists the plant as ground water keeps the substrate relatively warm through the winter months. When the flower does open, it is often to breezes still devoid of most insect life. To attract the few available pollinators the skunk cabbage produces an irresistible odor that is a vile mix of carrion, skunk spray, and onion. All of this hurry to bloom is not without cost — skunk cabbage flowers hit by frost die easily, leaving behind a rotting, stinking mass of wasted vegetation.

Perhaps only a naturalist could say "Bless the skunk cabbage and the swamps it frequents." There are better reasons for protecting wetlands. Yet, despite mud and stinks, it's worthwhile to fold open the inrolled edges of the skunk cabbage spathe to see that round, alien-looking spathe covered with lumps of male and female flowers. As long as we have swamps and skunk cabbage in forgotten woods, there will be hope even in the harshest winter blast.

February - March   Wooded swamps

18

Skunk Cabbage　　*Symplocarpus foetidus*

Indian Pipes   *Monotropa uniflora* L.

The white, waxen flowering stems of the Indian Pipe, rising mysteriously out of the forest mold, have led to its other common, if gory, name: *Corpse-plant*. Long associated with death and decay, and often confused with a mushroom because of its lack of green chlorophyll (the standard test for most self-respecting plants,) the Indian pipe is but one player in an intricate living arrangement which science is just beginning to understand.

A small minority of flowering plants are unable to produce their own food through the process called photosynthesis. This action, made possible by the unique chlorophyll molecule, is basic to life as we know it. Dispensing with chlorophyll, a plant may become a *saprophyte* adopting the life-style of a fungus, feeding on dead organic matter common in the forest topsoil. Indian pipe, a relative of the Rhododendrons is one example — coral-root, an orchid, is another.

As understanding of the role of decomposing organisms in ecological systems grows, new relationships emerge. For example, scientists now know that fungi have as much in common with animals as with plants and are really a separate and no less important kingdom of life. Evidence shows that the Indian pipe has struck a natural bargain with a fungus known as a Bolete. The roots of the Indian pipe mingle with the Bolete hyphae (thread-like strands which form the fungus' underground body) and together they suck nourishment from decaying plant matter and the roots of trees.

This partnership in predation is not nearly so sinister as it sounds. Similar studies point to the mutual dependence of fungi and many higher plants. Thus, the Indian pipe is a fitting symbol of the environmental dictum that "everything is connected to everything else," — and a good argument for preservation of even the most seemingly insignificant species of plant, animal, or fungus.

July - September   Woods

Indian Pipes   *Monotropa uniflora*

Columbine
Aquilegia canadensis L.

A plant of rich, rocky woods, columbine is not common on Cape Cod, but where the glacial hills around Buzzards Bay have been eroded into rocky hillsides, delicate clumps of this bright red flower can be found. Although its flowering parts have the characters of the buttercup family, there has been an intricate modification of the petals and sepals to better serve the fertilization of the flower. Each of the 5 petals, yellow inside and red outside, have stretched into a long, spreading spur. At the base of this spur nectar collects and attracts pollinators such as long-tongued moths and long-beaked hummingbirds. Pollen from the cluster of stamens that sticks out of the flower is brushed onto the heads of these animals to be taken to another flower.

Garden varieties of columbine come in many colors, and occassionally these flowers of European origin can be found growing along our roadsides, though they seldom stray far from the garden. The wild flower is daintier, its red blossoms hanging lightly from the tips of stems decked with rounded, dissected leaves. Although the mix of red and yellow in the flowers is unique, one can search for rarer all-yellow and white forms as well.

Columbine raises a number of delightful images. Those familiar with the Rocky Mountains think of alpine meadows strewn with the blue and white species common there. In New England the image is of secluded wooded dells. The Latin word *Aquila* appears in the scientific name, referring to the resemblance of the flower to an eagle's curled talon. Columbine itself is a reference to the dove, *Columba*, based on a fancied resemblance to five doves gathered around a water hole. A better New England name is "Meetinghouses", an imaginative vision that likens the uplifted spurs to the spires of church steeples. Lore going back to the days of the native Wampanoags speaks of a love potion concocted from the nectar and seeds of this plant. Dropped on the hand of your beloved, this concoction assured eternal bliss. (This legendary use, of course, led to that pop hit of the fifties, "Love Potion Columbine.")

May - June   Rich, rocky woods

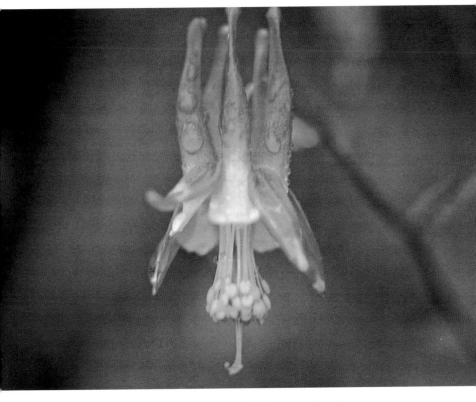

Wild Columbine   *Aquilegia canadensis*

Lambkill; Sheep Laurel   *Kalmia angustifolia* L.

A common, medium-sized shrub with thin evergreen leaves, lambkill grows in a variety of habitats, from coastal plain bogs to windswept mountain-tops. While most plants show an affinity for either dry or moist soil, lambkill refuses to be categorized, being quite at home on a dry oak hillside or a cultivated cranberry bog.

Lambkill is wild kin to our domestic azaleas and rhododendrons. From a scattered corymb along the side of the branchlet, one-inch wide pink to crimson flowers shaped like miniature parasols erupt in a display similar to its larger cousin, mountain laurel. Though flowering has peaked by late June, sporadic blossoms continue until October.

Within the cup-shaped flower (actually five petals fused as one) an interesting pollination mechanism can be observed. The pollen-bearing anthers of the ten stamens are embedded in a tiny pouch, ready to be sprung at the slightest touch of a bee. This hair-trigger device results in a spraying of pollen over the back of the potential pollinator. The unwitting courier then flies this precious gold dust to the next blossom, insuring cross-fertilization.

Known also as sheep or pig laurel, lambkill is not a true member of the Laurel family. The true laurels were used in ancient Greece in the original Olympics as winner's wreaths for the victorious athletes.

Lambkill's name derives from a less glorious origin than the Laurels; the foliage is toxic to grazing animals, causing paralysis and death in some cases. Domestic animals such as sheep, pigs and cattle seem more inclined to nibble this low shrub than wild animals.

The father of modern taxonomy, Carolus Linnaeus, named the genus of American laurels, including sheep and mountain laurel, *Kalmia*, after his dedicated young protege, Pehr Kalm. Kalm traveled extensively throughout North America in the Eighteenth Century collecting and sending back to Europe plant specimens for study. No doubt one of Kalm's discoveries was the showy lambkill.

May-Sporadic to October   Wet to Dry Woods

Lambkill; Sheep Laurel *Kalmia angustifolia*

Ponds and Bogs

ONCE FILLED WITH IMPUNITY to create buildable upland, the ponds and bogs which checkerboard Cape Cod are finally being recognized and protected as the 'kidneys' of our groundwater supply system.

The land between deep water and upland, the transition zone known as wetlands, provides a valuable buffer between the constant onslaught of pollutants from development, such as nitrates, phosphates and hydrocarbons, and the sole-source aquifer which a large part of this region depends on for its drinking water.

Wetlands in the form of ponds and bogs also provide a valuable service in storm damage prevention and flood control by acting as repositories for storm water runoff and precipitation. By storing large amounts of water and slowly releasing it, wetlands act as downflow regulators of potential floodwaters.

Wildlife diversity is always great in or near wetland habitats. Ponds, bogs and wooded swamps provide food, cover and breeding habitat for a variety of flora and fauna, many listed as threatened or endangered species. According to the Massachusetts Natural Heritage Program, 22 plant species found in the broad peaty apron of coastal kettle ponds are rare in Massachusetts, with 10 rare species listed for acid bogs.

There are some six hundred freshwater ponds and lakes in southeastern Massachusetts. Many of these are coastal plain kettle ponds, ice age relics which provide acidic, peaty pondshores where such rarities as Plymouth gentian, redroot, thread-leaved sundew and New England boneset can be found.

Development and recreational pressures are relentless threats to this habitat, as a 'pondshore view' home eventually evolves into a private beach, pier or boat dock. Restricting pondshore development through tighter zoning control, open space acquisition and conservation restrictions are better long-range solutions than the landmark state Wetlands Protection Act, (WPA), which allows the filling of wetlands in some cases, and only conditions development projects in most others.

Acid bogs characterized by mats of sphagnum moss, cranberry, and leatherleaf are being converted daily to cultivated cranberry or blueberry bogs. This controversial conversion of a diversified natural system to a pesticide-laden monoculture is allowed in most cases under the state WPA but may be denied under stricter Federal measures.

Such uncommon and beautiful bog orchids as the rose pogonia, calopogon and arethusa may survive bog conversion, only to succumb to the pre-emergent herbicides such as Dichlobenil which are now widely used in cranberry cultivation. One thing is certain. As true upland becomes almost totally developed, increasing pressure will be brought to bear on marginal wetland areas. With only a tenuous hold on existence, the future for many of these plants (and the animals who live on them) depends on intelligent, long-range land planning now.

— mjd

White Water Lily

Rose Pogonia or Snakemouth

Redroot

Cranberry

Sundew

Jewelweed or Touch-me-not

Meadow Beauty

Rose Coreopsis

Pickerelweed

Cardinal Flower

White-fringed Orchid

White Water Lily   *Nymphaea odorata*   Ait.

Languid, sultry summer days often conjure up visions of barefoot children playing and fishing by a pondside gleaming with the brilliant blossoms of the white water lily. Its Latin name means 'Fragrant Water-nymph', an allusion to its refreshing, sweet odor and aquatic habitat.

The purity of the water lily's color and fragrance belies its ecological requirements. This is a plant of muddy-bottomed eutrophic ponds; oftentimes these waterbodies are depositories for road and septic run-off. The water lily thrives in the nitrates and phosphates which are the principal pollutants from poorly functioning septic systems, very green lawns and busy golfcourses. The result can be a shallow pond choked with aquatic weeds and algal blooms leading to acute oxygen deprivation. Ironic as it seems, this lovely wildflower is often an indicator of polluted water.

The white water lily is our most common pond lily, sporting 16-32 white or pink petals. The flowers open only when the sun is high and generally close by early afternoon. The familiar orbicular leaves float atop the water's surface, making great landing strips for spring peepers, wood frogs and dragonflies.

A thick root system lies beneath two to three feet of pond muck; oxygen is provided by way of a four-chambered stem, a kind of umbilical cord to the anaerobic world beneath the pond bottom. These substantial roots, called rhizomes, were eaten by Cape Indians, who dried and powdered them. They are relished by muskrats, who store large quantities in their lodges .

Henry D. Thoreau, the Concord sage, smoked dried water-lily stems as an adolescent and later wrote of his admiration for a plant which could produce such brilliance from the mire of a black pond bottom:

> *Growing in stagnant and muddy water, it bursts*
> *up so pure and fair to the eye and so sweet*
> *to the scent, as if to show us what purity*
> *and sweetness reside in, and can be extracted*
> *from, the slime and muck of earth. It sug-*
> *gests that the time may come when man's deeds*
> *will smell as sweet.*

June-September   Shallow Ponds

White Water Lily   *Nymphaea odorata*

Rose Pogonia; Snakemouth   *Pogonia ophioglossoides* L.

There are nearly 35,000 species of orchids world-wide, making them the world's second largest family of flowering plants (the grasses, *Poaceae*, are the largest). Few local species of this complex family can match the strange beauty of the so-called 'bog-orchids'. This acidic-peat loving trio includes the arethusa, (see Endangered section), grass-pink and rose pogonia.

All three species, including the pogonia, display a long-fringed lip with bright pink and yellow striping. This ragged lip gives the plant its other name, snakemouth. It acts as a 'honey guide' for potential pollinators, who emerge from the flower with a sticky-pack of pollen atop their heads. This *pollinia* pack may then be transferred, via the bumblebee express, onto the next flower's stigma, resulting in cross fertilization. Unlike its bog brethren, rose pogonia can also reproduce vegetatively, making it far more common than either grass pink or arethusa.

Rose pogonia grows in wet, acidic soils. In late June, a spear-like stem shoots up, unfurling a single, elliptic leaf. One or rarely two bright pink to white blossoms open atop the stem, displaying the curious open maw of the snakemouth.

There are sizable colonies of both rose pogonias and grass pinks in the miniature bogs which form in dune hollows at the Cape Cod National Seashore or Sandy Neck. Old cranberry bogs and even those in active production are also good places to look for these ornate beauties. Bog orchids were so common in the late nineteenth century that young girls were paid a penny a pound to rid the bogs of these "weeds".

Bog orchids are rare in many places, with arethusa having nearly disappeared completely. Their attractiveness makes them vulnerable to collectors, children and transplant-hopefuls.

Though rose pogonia grows locally in considerable numbers, the colonies themselves are scattered and susceptible to alteration in hydrology due to construction impacts, wetland draining and conversion of old cranberry bogs back to commercial operation.

Mid-June-Early July   Wet Acidic Bogs; Sphagnum

Rose Pogonia *Pogonia ophioglossoides*

Redroot   *Lachnanthes caroliniana*   (Lam.) Dandy

Redroot is one of twenty-two plant species listed by the Massachusetts Natural Heritage Program as being endangered, threatened or of special concern found growing in the peaty sand aprons of coastal kettle ponds. Water levels fluctuate dramatically in these small water bodies, and in years of very high water, plants like redroot lie dormant beneath the ground. Flowering being a rather tiresome business, botanists believe these high-water periods are vital for energy restoration to the plants' perennial rhizomes.

In years when water levels reveal a pond's wide apron, the dusky yellow flowers of redroot may be seen in a few kettle ponds between Barnstable and Brewster. The cyme of wooly flowers is alluded to in its Greek scientific name, Lachne (wool) and Anthos (flower).

Redroot is the sole eastern North American representative of the Bloodwort Family, the majority of species being found in central and South America. Most share redroot's bright-colored juice. Its range is a disjunct one; from the deep South, where it is common, continuing north to Virginia, where it skips over to Delaware. With the exception of a small colony recently located in Nova Scotia, Cape Cod marks the northern limit of its range.

Redroot has a nondescript mien, with its half-opened flowers arranged in unspectacular style. Perhaps its gaudiest aspect is the mercurochrome-red juice found in the stem and roots. This scarlet sap readily stains fingers and clothing and was historically used for blood disorders, (it was not unusual under the Doctrine of Signatures to utilize any bright red or orange juiced plant for diseases of the blood, the species having been literally 'red-flagged' by Providence to be used in this manner).

This species' rarity lies in the scarcity of its preferred habitat, bogs and kettle pond shores, and by the fact that it is at the fringe of its range. Plants, like animals, don't compete as well on the geographical edge of their distribution. Redroot is a Child of Dixie and prefers steamier climactic conditions than what southeastern Massachusetts offers. It can indeed be a prolific encroacher in cranberry bogs south of New England, and is reviled and yanked as a pernicious weed by some southern growers.

July-August   Bogs; Wet Meadows

Redroot   *Lachnanthes caroliniana*

Cranberry
Vaccinium macrocarpon Ait.
V. oxycoccus L.

No other cultivated or wild fruit plays as prominent a role in this region's folklore and economy as the cranberry. The neat quiltwork of crimson bogs liberally decorate the landscape of Barnstable County. As an agricultural crop, cranberry is enjoying a strong resurgence due to a burgeoning demand overseas for mixed fruit-cranberry juice products. As a result, more wetlands are being converted to cultivated bogs, damaging wildlife habitat and hydraulically connected water bodies. A serious fish kill on the Coonamessett River in Falmouth has been attributed to improper pesticide application on cranberry bogs.

The cranberry has a long history of use dating to before the Advent of European colonists. New England Native Americans stewed the sour fruit with honey or maple syrup. At Plimoth settlement, the fruit was used not only as food, but as a medicinal remedy for a host of afflictions. The famed herbalist John Josselyn wrote in 1672, "They are excellent against the scurvy. They are also good to allay the fervour of hot Diseases. The Indians and the English use them much"

Wild cranberries are still quite common in southeastern Massachusetts, with the untamed fruit being just as robust as the cultivated, without the pesticides. Any low peaty area which is moist most of the year and gets plenty of sunlight is a likely spot to search for this famed tart berry.

Like many members of the Heath Family, the cranberry is a low evergreen sub-shrub which tends to creep, vine-like, over the damp peat of a bog. There are actually two species of cranberry found in this area, named rather unimaginatively large cranberry and small cranberry. The physical differences between the two are slight, the large obviously bearing bigger fruit. Small, sometimes known as 'wren's egg', cranberry is uncommon. Its egg-shaped berry is more tart than its larger cousin, making it less palatable right off the vine.

For those who would venture into a wild cranberry bog to partake of this fruit, watch for the telltale hole which indicates the tenancy of the Sphagnosis worm. Uninvaded fruit can be made into a delicious jelly by boiling one quart of berries with a pint of water for a half hour, straining the mixture through a sieve, then boiling again with a pound of sugar. This mix should be poured into a mold and set to cool.

June   Wet Peaty Ground

Cranberry   *Vaccinium macrocarpon*

Sundew:

Thread-leaved	*Drosera filiformis* Raf.
Round-leaved	*D. rotundifolia* L.
Spatulate-leaved	*D. intermedia* Hayne

There are plants which capture the imagination not for their beauty or fragrance but for uniqueness of form and function. The insectivorous sundew is one of these.

The damp acidic sands and peats of the coastal areas of southeastern Massachusetts provide prime habitat for three species of sundew. They are distinguished by the shape of their leaves, ranging from the circular leaf of the round-leaved to the long, string-like blades of the thread-leaved, with the spatulate-leaved shaped somewhere between the two. It's not the form of the leaf which marks this plant as special, but its eating habits.

Covering the leaves of the sundew are red-tipped glandular hairs which exude a viscid liquid. Acting on the same principal as fly-paper, the sundew ensnares any hapless insect which should alight. The sticky hairs then cover the bug over and enzymes are secreted which digest the plant's prey. Scientific studies show that the nitrogen derived from the insect is then stored in the perennial root system, to be used for future flowering and seed formation.

It is no accident that the sundew, as well as other insectivorous plants like the pitcher plant and venus fly-trap, grow in nutrient-poor habitats like acidic bogs and peats; insectivory provides an additional source of sustenance needed in such harsh environments.

Sundews have been used in a variety of ways for centuries in Europe. In Scandinavia, the glandular leaves are used like rennett to thicken milk. In southern Europe, a ruby-red liqueur is distilled from the glutinous droplets. The scientific name, *Drosera*, is from the Greek *Droseros* meaning 'dewy ' or 'misty'.

All three sundew species are locally common on the Cape and Islands, though the thread-leaved is listed as a Watch List species by the Massachusetts Natural Heritage Program. While the 'thread-dew' is relatively common in southern Massachusetts, its national range is quite limited. Certainly the growing recreational pressures on the Cape's pondshores could have dire consequences for even healthy populations of this fascinating plant.

June-August   Wet Peat: Sandy Pondshores

Sundew   *Drosera filiformis*

Jewelweed; Touch-Me-Not   *Impatiens capensis*   Meerb

The pendant flowers of jewelweed or touch-me-not is a common, but always welcome sight along streams, creeks and other wetlands in mid-summer. Its many common names bespeak a history of human use dating to pre-colonial times. Snapweed, balsam and even ladies' earrings are some of the handles attached to this attractive and useful plant.

The sac-like orange flowers hang down from the leaf axils, an open invitation to bees, butterflies and hummingbirds to try the nectar found within the long curved spur at the rear of the blossom.

The actual coloration can vary, with a light orange, relatively unspotted form occurring on Cape Cod, *(forma immaculata)*. The more common form, consisting of a darker orange with chestnut mottling around the throat, is found throughout eastern Massachusetts, with yellow and white flowered plants rarely encountered.

This species, like all members of the *Impatiens* genus, is a watery-juiced annual which bears explosive seed capsules. A walk through a jewelweed patch in September can set off a volley of nut-like seeds in all directions. Its Latin name derives from the impatient nature of its seed dispersal.

The yellow-orange stem juice is legendary for its effects as an antidote to poison ivy and fungal infections such as ringworm and athletes foot. Native American uses included a balm for aches. It was mixed with hog's grease to make a salve for bruises. John Josselyn wrote, "there is not a more sovereign remedy for bruises of what kind so ever."

Jewelweed is found throughout the eastern United States, and reversing the usual trend, has established itself in Europe where it is known as American jewelweed.

June-September   Wet Ground; Streamsides

Spotted Jewelweed *Impatiens capensis*

Meadow-beauty

Rhexia virginica   L.
R. mariana   L.

There exist wildflowers which, despite ornate structure and vivid hue, generally escape the attention of the casual public and are noticed only by those who toil in cranberry bogs or botanize in wetlands. Such a wildflower is the meadow-beauty or deergrass.

Meadow-beauty grows in damp areas on the edges of bogs, wet meadows and sandy areas around kettle ponds. Two species of meadow-beauty occur on Cape Cod; the Virginia meadow-beauty, with four hot-pink to magenta petals, and the Maryland meadow-beauty, with light-pink to white petals. The Maryland species is by far the rarest, and is listed as Endangered by the Massachusetts Natural Heritage Program.

At the beginning of 1986, less than ten locations for Maryland meadow-beauty had been documented in all of New England. Its presence on Cape Cod represents the very northern fringe of its national range. The main impacts on this plant are recreational, with populations feeling pressure from four-wheelers and a proliferation of private beaches.

Meadow-beauty is also called deer-grass because of its preferential status as browse for deer and moose. The plant's Latin name, *Rhexia*, means 'rupture', an apparent allusion to its ancient qualities as a healer of wounds.

Thoreau admired the Meadow-beauty, not only for its flaming blossoms, but for its unique, urn-shaped seed capsule, which he likened to "perfect little cream pitchers".

Two new prolific colonies of Maryland meadow-beauty were found in Brewster in 1986. The land owners agreed to coordinate with the Nature Conservancy in its rare plant registry program, allowing a kind of conservation buffer zone around the Meadow-beauty colonies. A small but important part of Cape Cod's flora has been preserved, at least for now.

July-September   Wet Sand and Peat

Virginia Meadow Beauty   *Rhexia virginica*

Maryland Meadow Beauty   *Rhexia mariana*

43

Rose Coreopsis   *Coreopsis rosea*   Nutt.

A dainty and delicate member of the coastal plain kettle pond community, rose coreopsis looks much like a diminutive pink mayweed or daisy. It can colonize by the hundreds around the sandy apron of a Cape Cod pondshore. Because of its sensitivity to habitat alteration, the vigor of a rose coreopsis colony is a good barometer of the pondshore community's general health and its ability to absorb local human impacts.

Rose coreopsis, also known as pink tickseed, is a perennial herb which spreads by subterranean runners called rhizomes. Its flowerheads, like most members of the Composite or Aster Family, are composed of the outer, sterile ray flowers and the fertile,inner flowers which form the disk. The eight ray flowers in rose coreopsis are colored in various shades of pink, rarely producing a pure white form. The linear leaves are paired or sometimes whorled on the one to two foot high stem.

The shape of its short, squat seed or achene gives both a colloquial name, tickseed, and its scientific name, *Coreopsis*, which is Greek for 'bug-like'. Ironically, while many species in the *Coreopsis* genus have hooked achenes which can act like hitchiking ticks, *Coreopsis rosea*'s are hookless and smooth, unable to catch a free ride.

Rose coreopsis has a disjunct range nationally, with local populations sporadically reported from Cape Cod south to eastern Maryland. Geologists theorize that many coastal plain plant populations were inundated by the rise in sea level with the melting of the last great glaciers 12,000 years ago. As a result, outliers of what was once the Atlantic coastal plain, such as Cape Cod, Block Island, Martha's Vineyard, Nantucket and Long Island became remnant habitat for plants dependent on the broad, peaty margins of coastal kettle ponds.

An interesting enclave of the Atlantic coastal plain exists in the Tusket Valley of Yarmouth County, Nova Scotia. Here is found Canada's only occurrence of Plymouth gentian and rose Coreopsis, both of which are nationally endangered in that country.

July-September   Damp Peaty Pondshores

44

Rose Coreopsis *Coreopsis rosea*

Pickerelweed

Pontederia cordata   L.

The place to look for pickerelweed is where water meets land. In late summer, a striking blue-violet ring of this vigorous plant forms around ponds, lakes and other slow-moving bodies of water.

The eye-catching spike of six-petaled flowers and the solitary, arrow-shaped leaf makes pickerelweed one of the most familiar of wetland emergents. It is also a prodigious consumer of water-borne pollutants such as nitrates,phosphates and heavy metals.

This ability is shared by a close relative, water hyacinth, which is used extensively in the South for advanced treatment of sewage plant effluent. Perhaps pickerelweed can someday be similarly used as a living filter for septic treatment plants on Cape Cod.

As the floral spike becomes heavy with seed, its head lowers into the water, where the starchy fruit is eaten by waterfowl and muskrats. This fruit was occasionally ground into flour in Colonial times to stretch supplies of wheat or rye flour. The young leaves were boiled as greens.

July-October   Ponds and Lakes

Pickerelweed   *Pontederia cordata*

Cardinal Flower   *Lobelia cardinalis*   L.

There are few truly red flowers. Shades of pink and salmon, magenta and rose, carmine and lake are common enough, but true flaming reds are restricted to a privileged college that includes the cardinal flower. So seering is its color that photographic film tends to record it in an oddly vivid manner — as if the color were bleeding out of the photo back into the real world.

Like other flowers of scarlet hue — columbine, bee balm, trumpet honeysuckle — cardinal flower has a tubular shape which invites pollination by hummingbirds. The vision-blurring beat of a humming-bird's wings requires a great deal of energy for so small a creature, and the concentrated sugars of flower nectar are just the right fuel for its flights. Bright reds and oranges are the colors used by plants to signal that their flowers are designed to accomodate the soda-straw beak of the hummingbird, but nature doesn't always hold true to type, and pink or white cardinal flowers can be found.

Both the color of the flower and its miter-like shape refer to the trappings of the Roman Catholic hierarchy. Like other members of the *Lobelia* genus, the flower has two lobes lifted upward and three pointed down, and the anthers are united into a tube around the style, looking like a part of the petals. Growing 2 to 4 feet high, with dark green leaves and fleshy stems with an acrid juice, the plant is a stunning surprise amid the thick green vegetation and otherwise muted colors of late summer stream bank thickets.

So surprising is the cardinal flower's firecracker red that it moved even our most famous naturalists to uncharacteristic behaviors. Roger Tory Peterson, that otherwise objective chronicler of the minutiae of bird and plant identification, added a rare bit of editorial comment when, in his *Field Guide to Wildflowers,* he noted that it was chosen "America's Favorite." And Thoreau, that champion of a sensitive approach to nature's phenomenon, said that the plant reminded him of his sins and confessed that he plucked it time and again. Common enough along our thickly wooded streams, we would do best *not* to emulate Thoreau in this regard, leaving the cardinal flower for the hummingbirds which attend it so well.

August - September   Wooded stream banks

48

Cardinal Flower　　*Lobelia cardinalis*

White-fringed Orchid

Platanthera blephariglottis   (Willdenow) Lindley

The 'rein' orchids comprise an interesting genus whose species exhibit spikes of delicate winged flowers, (see bog candles). The term 'rein' probably alludes to the strap-like lower lip or long curved spur of the individual flowers. Rein orchids generally are found in damp boggy soils or rich woods. Five species are found on Cape Cod; all are uncommon to rare.

Perhaps the most frequently encountered rein orchid in the region is the white-fringed. An impressive plant sometimes topping three feet in height, this species displays anywhere from twenty to thirty, half-inch flowers in a dense spike. The color of the flowers is a dazzling milk-white except for the long spur, which is colored by the nectar stored within it. Only moths with very long proboscises are able to reach the nectary. As they probe deeply within the spur, the sticky *pollinia* adheres to the insect's thorax and is carried to the next plant in a critical sequence which insures greater health and vigor through cross-pollination.

The white-fringed orchid enjoys wet peats and bogs with filtered sunlight. It may be found in more wooded areas than other wetland orchids. While it is still locally scattered through the entire Cape area, its numbers in recent years seem to be declining. It does appear that new colonies of this orchid are extremely uncommon.

Flowering in New England begins in mid-June and stretches to August in the northern Maritime Provinces. A larger variety occurs in the southern U.S.

June-July   Peaty Bogs; Wet Meadow

White-fringed Orchid *Platanthera blephariglottis*

Sandplains:
Heaths and Pine Barrens

Sandplains are typified by sandy, excessively-drained soils with a plant community described as *xeric*, or able to withstand the dessicating extremes of desert-like conditions. These are tough plants indeed, but they're no match for a new subdivision or burger stand. The open, level sandplain heaths and pine barrens of Cape Cod are under attack as that most valuable of commodities, buildable upland.

A corollary to development is fire suppression. Both sandplain heaths and pine barrens are products of fire, which is instrumental in keeping areas open and free from woody invaders such as the tree oaks, red cedar and bush honeysuckle. Without the purging effect of fire, succession blots out the many unique, rare species which inhabit these areas. Massachusetts Natural Heritage data shows nine rare plant species endemic to pine barrens and sixteen found in sandpain heaths and grasslands. While only ten per cent of the state's land is labled sandy, a disproportionate number of rare plants and animals depend on this harsh environment for survival.

The open heaths dotted with the curious mounds of broom crowberry, bearberry and golden heather can best be enjoyed in the outer Cape towns of Truro and Wellfleet. One classic heath area can be viewed from the entrance road into the Cape Cod National Seashore Headquarters in Wellfleet.

Just off Cape, the pine barrens of Plymouth and Carver, largely within the Myles Standish State Forest, is the third largest in the United States. This area provides the ample habitat size needed to sustain breeding Eastern bluebirds, whipporwills and prairie warblers as well as substantial populations of wild lupine, blazing stars, birdfoot violet and wood lily. Characteristic stands of pine barrens habitat are also found in Sandwich, Barnstable and Brewster.

Woody succession, development, fire suppression and even occasional conversion to monocultures such as white pine plantations, are chronic threats to this austere, yet critically-important ecosystem.

— mjd

Poverty Grass

Bearberry

Frostweed

Wild Lupine

Ladies-tresses

Birdfoot Violet

Stiff or Frost Aster

Prickly Pear Cactus

Wild Indigo

Yellow Thistle

Butterflyweed

Broom Crowberry

Blue Curls

Sickle-leaved Golden Aster

Wood Lily

New England Blazing Star

Poverty Grass, Beach Heather   *Hudsonia tomentosa*   Nutt.
H. ericoides   L.

On Henry Thoreau's last trip to Cape Cod in 1857, he watched expectantly for a plant which for him represented the 'transition' from mainland soils and vegetation to the sandy coastal counties of Plymouth and Barnstable. He was looking for the low, moundlike shrub called poverty grass or beach heather.

In a Journal entry dated June 19, Thoreau wrote "The poverty-grass emits a common sweetish scent as you walk over the fields. It blossoms on the edges first. You meet with it in Plymouth as you approach the peculiar soil of the Cape." Poverty grass is a mound-forming evergreen subshrub which acts as an important erosion control species on coastal dunes and banks. It is unfortunately very sensitive to off-road recreational impacts, where a single pass by a vehicle over a mound of *Hudsonia* can cause permanent damage.

There are actually two closely related species of Poverty Grass. They can be told apart, though the differences are subtle. *Hudsonia tomentosa*, called beach heather, has a white-wooly, tightly scaled foliage with yellow flowers on very short stalks. It is more common in sand dunes and coastal gravels. Golden heather, *Hudsonia ericoides*, is a much greener plant with spreading, needle-like leaves. The bright yellow flowers are on long stalks.

Golden heather is more common in coastal areas on eastern Cape Cod but also occurs in inland scrub pine habitats of Plymouth County and even on mountain tops in central New Hampshire. To blur the distinction between the two species even more is an intermediate hybrid variety with characteristics of both which can occasionally be found on the lower Cape.

The Hudsonias are shade-intolerant plants which use a root toxin to discourage herbaceous competition from robbing the precious sunlight. Exposed to wind, salt and sun, they have evolved small, needle-like leaves and a low profile to retard desiccation.

The bright yellow ringlets of flowers decorate the dunes and heaths in June. Very large and impressive colonies can be seen in the interdune areas of Sandy Neck in Barnstable, where the characteristic round mounds resemble great yellow-green tortoises half-burrowed into the sand. As an important erosion control plant, poverty grass plays both a utilitarian and aesthetic role in heathland ecology.

Late May-June   Dunes and Heaths

Golden Heather   *Hudsonia ericoides*

Poverty Grass, Beach Heather   *Hudsonia tomentosa*

Bearberry; Hog-Cranberry   *Arctostaphylos uva-ursi*   L.

There are few plants which not only survive the austere conditions of heathland and dune, but actually thrive in it. Bearberry, or hog cranberry as it is known locally, is one of these.

Bearberry is a handsome vine-like shrub which can cover an entire dune with its evergreen leaves here on the Cape as well as rocky mountain ledges in the Arctic. It seems wherever growing conditions are the harshest, bearberry flourishes. It combats the desiccating effects of salt-laden wind and sun with a thick, waxy cuticle on the leaves which retards water loss and gives them a shiny, almost luminescent appearance. It also knows how to stay out of the wind by hugging the ground, rarely growing over six inches tall.

A tenacious trailer, bearberry is one of the most important erosion control species and is often cultivated for that reason. Displaying urn-shaped white and pink-tipped flowers in late April, it is one of the earliest of the heathland species to bloom. With a little botanic sleuthing, the rarely-encountered autumnal-flowering bearberry (*Arctostaphylos uva-ursi* f. heterochroma) can be found on eastern Cape Cod and Nantucket in October and November. This unusual flowering form is the same species as the normal white-flowered plant, yet its blossoms are a deep magenta and the calyx is distinctly longer than the typical variety.

Bearberry's use as a medicine, tobacco substitute and astringent tea has been documented since the thirteenth century. Its properties as a reliever of renal disorders and as a diuretic made it well known in the late 1800's, when it was marketed as "Uva-Ursi". It was even popularly used as a laxative well into this century.

Its long history of human uses has given bearberry a legion of names. These include hog cranberry (an oft-used moniker on the Cape), mealyberry, bear grape, foxberry, crowberry, Sagachomi and in the far West, kinnikinick , where its leaves have been smoked by the Indians for centuries.

As the majority of these names seem to attest, the bright red berries are relished by wildlife, but the mealy, tasteless fruit makes for poor human fare.

May   Coastal Sands; Dunes

58

Bearberry; Hog-Cranberry *Arctostaphylos uva-ursi*

Frostweed   *Helianthemum canadense*   (L.) Michx.

The tough aspect of the Cape's sandplains and pine barrens is sometimes softened by the delicate presence of frostweed.

Topping a one to two foot high wand-like stem, the solitary flower is composed of five lemon yellow petals. Inside and contrasting nicely against the petals are numerous stamens capped with bright orange anthers.

The flowers are large, over an inch across. Each bud will flower but once, in bright sunshine only, then drop its petals. This dependence on direct sun for blossoming gave it the Greek scientific name *Helianthemum*, meaning sun flower.

Frostweed also bears flowers which do not open, but actually self-fertilize to form fruit. These cleistogamous flowers hardly match their petaliferous kin for beauty, but they do get the job of fertilization and seed formation accomplished without a great expenditure of energy. Frostweed's habitat of dry roadsides and gravelly areas drains on the plant's energy reserves, so self-fertilizing flowers are an efficient way to save resources.

There are four species of frostweed in the area, all resembling to some extent the common species described in the narrative. One, bushy rockrose, is rare and listed by the Massachusetts Natural Heritage Program as a species of Special Concern. Unlike frostweed, it forms roundish colonies of stems and is lower than other members of the genus.

Frostweed gets its name from the tendency of the stem to crack and exude sap, which forms ice crystals in the late autumn air.

June-August   Sand Barrens; Dry Areas

Frostweed   *Helianthemum canadense*

Wild Lupine   *Lupinus perennis*   L.

There are some wildflowers which, due to vividness of color and attractiveness of design, look like refugees from a cultivated garden. It is difficult to believe that the harsh, nutrient-poor soil of the sandplain and pine barren could produce the lush foliage and brilliant blue-purple floral spikes of wild lupine.

Lupinus perennis is the northeast's only species of native lupine. There are dozens of lupines in the western U.S., including the closely-related Texas bluebonnet (*Lupinus subcarnosus*).

All lupines are characterized by a terminal spike of brightly-colored pea flowers and leaves with a distinctive 'wagon-wheel' whorl of 7-11 leaflets. This leaflet pattern is an adaptation, acting as a kind of radar dish to catch the full rays of the sun. The leaves actually follow the sun in its daily migration across the summer sky in order to maximize photosynthesis. This ability to 'track' the sunshine gave it the popular name, sun dial.

Lupine derives both its common and scientific names from a misnomer. *Lupinus* is Latin for wolf, the name attributed to this plant because, as Wood's 1855 Classbook of Botany stated, "it overruns the field and devours its fertility."

Nothing could be farther from the truth. Wild lupine, like all legumes, fixes nitrogen from the atmosphere into the soil using a kind of bacteria in its root nodules. It thus enhances, not decreases, nutrient levels in areas where it grows.

Wild lupine is nowhere as common as it once was. Development, loss of open areas due to natural succession and fire suppression, and even over-picking have taken a real toll on this handsome species. The Massachusetts Natural Heritage Program has recently placed the wild lupine on its Watch List, a preliminary warning list for species whose numbers or habitat appear to be changing for the worse.

The upper Cape still supports good numbers of wild lupine, with extensive colonies found along the Cape Cod Canal's sandy spoilands. Once encountered, a field of these beautiful wildflowers in full bloom is impressive indeed. Resist the very real temptation to gather a bouquet for the table vase and remember to leave this 'wolf' of the sandplains alone!

Late May-Early June   Sandy Fields

Wild Lupine   *Lupinus perennis*

Ladies-Tresses

Spiranthes spp.

While asters and goldenrods are stealing everyone's attention in late summer and early fall, the delicate white coils of the ladies-tresses quietly appear in dry to moist fields throughout the area.

The floral arrangement is unique, with the gossamer-like flowers braided spirally around the stem, an interesting intertwining which gives it another common name, pearl twist.

As in all orchids, the pollination scheme for the ladies-tresses is arcane and at times difficult to accomplish. The flower spikes mature from the bottom up; the immature flowers towards the top produce pollen disks which are cemented onto the backs of bumblebees. The bees then descend the spike to the fully-open, mature flowers, where the pollen disk is rubbed onto the receptive stigma.

If all of that goes without a hitch, the fertilized ovary will form a ribbed capsule containing millions of spore-like seeds. A germinated seed takes three years to produce a flowering stem, a much shorter time period than other orchids (ladies-slippers take ten to fifteen years).

There are four species of ladies-tresses found in our area, all somewhat resembling each other. With close examination, each species can usually be told apart, though hybridization can make identification difficult.

Little ladies-tresses (*Spiranthes tuberosa*) is the smallest, with tiny flowers twining in a single rank about the stem. It grows in dry, sand plains and gravelly waste lots and is on the state Watch List.

Slender ladies-tresses (*S. lacera* var. *gracilis*) is a beautiful member of this group, with a graceful, wand-like floral spike and a distinctive spiral staircase of flowers, (giving it another descriptive name, screw-auger). Each floret has a single green stripe on the gaping lip, as well as a lovely fragrance.

Spring ladies-tresses (*S. vernalis*) is by far the scarcest species of *Spiranthes* in the area. Just three Barnstable County sites have been recorded for this robust, two to three foot high plant. Along with its relatively coarse aspect, spring ladies-tresses has a very leafy stem and a yellow lip. It is listed on the state rare list as a Special Concern species.

The commonest and best known is nodding ladies-tresses, (*S. cernua*), named for its humped, pearl-white flowers which seem to nod down on the spike. It sometimes flowers into November.

August-October   Dry to Moist Meadows; Fields

Slender Ladies-Tresses
Spiranthes gracilis

Nodding Ladies-Tresses
Spiranthes cernua

65

Birdfoot Violet   *Viola pedata*   L.

Violets have long been among the most fabled of wildflowers. In Greek mythology, Io, the daughter of Atlas, fled the amorous advances of Apollo by hiding in the woods. Dianna, Goddess of the Hunt, took pity on her and changed her to a violet. The "Dies violaris" of Ancient Rome was a day to decorate the graves of loved ones with flowers, most commonly violets. Colonial herbalists used the roots as an emetic and purgative and the heart-shaped leaves as a cure for cardiac problems.

The allure of violets is as strong today as it was in ancient times. There are few flowers as warmly welcomed as a harbinger of spring, with some species flowering in early April. While most violets have finished their blossoming by June, some will have a reprise flowering season in the fall.

There are no less than a dozen species of wild violet in our area, most native, but a few common garden escapes, such as the handsome Confederate violet (*Viola papilionacea* f. *albiflora*).

Most blue violets seem to enjoy a dry habitat while white ones are more often found in wet to damp areas. The few yellow violets which may be in our area prefer rocky woods and trails.

Perhaps the handsomest wild violet is the birdfoot or sand violet. Unlike the 'bonnet' arrangement of other violets' petals, the birdfoot has a more open, flatter profile, somewhat like its close relative, the pansy. At the center of the flower, bright orange stamens, unseen in other violet species, protrude conspicuously. The five petals display uniform shades of blue, purple or an exquisite lavender here in New England, while further south the flowers are bicolored.

This seemingly delicate wildflower grows in the most hostile of soils; along sandy roadsides, railroad tracks and sterile fields. Because of development, fire suppression, off-road vehicle destruction and overpicking, this once common Cape flower is now declining. It would be a significant blow to lose these brightly-colored daubs of lavender, which do such an admirable job of decorating our otherwise drab road shoulders or sandy waste lots.

May-October   Sandy Fields; Roadsides

Birdfoot Violet *Viola pedata*

Stiff or Frost Aster   *Aster linariifolius*   L.

As the denouement of the flowering season begins in early September, dry roadsides and fields seem to suddenly be carpeted with the lavender heads of the stiff aster. Taken as an individual plant, this species is not much to look at. However, the sight of a whole meadow of this lovely aster at the height of its blossoming is an autumnal treat.

While many aster species hybridize, making individual identification difficult, the stiff aster is readily distinguished by its rigid mien and stiff, linear leaves. It is a colonial plant, with many stems emanating from a subterranean rhizome.

The color of the ray flowers is also different from most other asters, showing a delightful light blue-violet or rarely pure white. A shared trait with other asters is the golden color of the disk flowers, which turn bronze with age.

Unlike most other plants in this book, the stiff aster is more common now than in the nineteenth century, when it was listed as rare in some botany texts. The asters represent a large genus, with over 150 species found in North America. Most have showy, radiate flower heads from which they derive the common and scientific name, *Aster*, Greek for star.

The asters offer welcome color at a time of the season when most other flowers are fast fading. It is not unusual to see this species, once known as the frost aster, still in flower well into November. Its prowess as a late bloomer is retold in an obscure stanza from the late 1800's:

> *Perhaps-ah! well, we cannot tell if truly it be so;*
> *I but repeat the legend sweet, and only this I know-*
> *That in the prime of Christmas-time,*
> *the Christ's sweet flowers blow.*

August-October   Heaths; Dry Fields

68

Stiff Aster *Aster linariifolius*

Prickly Pear Cactus   *Opuntia humifusa*   Raf.

The word 'cactus' generally conjures up images of the Southwest, with cowboys, Gila monsters and giant saguaro cacti set in a desert motif. It comes as a surprise to many that southern New England has a native cactus—the well-known prickly pear.

Reaching the northern limit of its range in eastern Massachusetts, there still remain a few questionably native colonies of this exotic-looking species, primarily on the lower Cape. Other sites in Massachusetts include a healthy population on Nantucket's Coatue Point and several probable transplants in Worcester County. Prickly pear's rarity in Massachusetts has earned it Special Concern status on the state rare plant list.

One reason for its scarcity is its attractiveness, which makes prickly pear a prime target for home gardeners and nurserymen. The stems are made up of flattened oval segments, which tend to sprawl over the ground. From the edges of the new growth large buds form, soon opening to spectacular, brilliant yellow flowers. The red fruit for which the plant is named is juicy and delicious, especially after chilling. Its other name, Indian fig, attests to its historical use by early Native Americans. The eastern variety of prickly pear lacks the sharp spines of its western counterparts, but it is armed with nearly invisible barb-like bristles known as glochids. If the stem or fruit of a plant are handled without gloves, the glochids imbed themselves into the skin and sting like a nettle. Their size makes them difficult to extricate. Those who have experienced both generally prefer the visible spines of the western prickly pear to the eastern's invisible stingers.

July-August   Sandy Fields; Dunes

Prickly Pear Cactus *Opuntia humifusa*

Wild Indigo   *Baptisia tinctoria*   (L.) R.Br.

In late June an amazing transformation takes place in sandy, sterile soil all over southeastern Massachusetts. From an asparagus-like main shoot, a round bushy plant sprouts and flourishes, sometimes in prolific numbers. Taking a comparatively short time to grow to considerable size, it soon attains a girth of three feet across and is covered with hundreds of yellow blossoms. Wild indigo now dominates the dry waste lots of our area.

Although resembling a shrub, wild indigo is completely herbaceous, dying back down at the end of the growing season and arising every June from a perennial rhizome. The clover-like leaves and pea flowers identify it as a member of the Legume or Pulse family, which is good news for the impoverished soil it usually grows in. All members of this family have the ability to introduce atmospheric nitrogen into the soil, using a special bacteria found in the root nodules.

This juicy, succulent plant is cloaked in an over-all bluish-green hue. Its roots and watery stem were once used in the manufacture of deep blue indigo dye, though all references seem to indicate a lack of quality in the product. Not surprisingly, its scientific name, *Baptisia*, is Greek for 'to dye'.

Another reported use was preparing the succulent shoots like asparagus by repeated boilings. This is not advised as livestock poisoning has been attributed to grazing of this species.

In September, the entire plant blackens and dies, breaks off at ground level and rolls over the windy heaths like an eastern counterpart to the tumbleweed. The seed pods rattle as the plant rolls, giving it the colloquial name, rattle-weed. Farmers once tied these dried plants to the collars of plough horses to ward off biting insects, hence another old name - 'sho-fly-weed'.

June-July   Dry Sterile Fields

Wild Indigo *Baptisia tinctoria*

Yellow Thistle   *Cirsium horridulum*   Michx.

The Thistles represent one of the most reviled family of plants found in North America. In some western states there has actually been legislation passed to encourage landowners to rid their fields of the obnoxious pest before seed set. Pulling thistle is a hated chore to which many mid-western farm families can attest.

Yet there is one species of local thistle which is found only sporadically and actually lends a touch of class to shores, fields and salt marshes all along the Atlantic coastal plain - the yellow thistle. Aside from the large golden flowerheads, an uncommon color for thistles, this species differs from its brethren by its retiring growing habits. It rarely makes a pest of itself. Never really common except on Martha's Vineyard, yellow thistle is hardly the prolific colonizer for which the other purple species are notorious.

Most thistles are armed with sharp spines on the leaf tips, yellow's well-armed foliage being no exception. Yet the three inch wide flowerhead, looking like a shaving brush made from porcupine quills, is soft and silky to the touch. Yellow thistle, like most of its spiny brethren, is a biennial. The first year cycle produces only a ground-hugging basal rosette of leaves, with the flowering stem coming the second and last year of life. At senescence, thousands of fluffy seeds are borne on the wind. Thistle seed is a favorite of birds, most particularly the American goldfinch, which relishes it as food and nesting material.

An excellent emergency food, the young leaves (sans spines!), root and inner stem of thistles are tasty boiled and salted like spinach. They have been used historically in decoctions to ease vascular complaints, a trait for which it derives its scientific name *Cirsium* meaning 'swollen vein'.

Late May-August   Coastal Fields

Yellow Thistle *Cirsium horridulum*

Butterfly-weed   *Asclepias tuberosa*   L.

The great Roman naturalist, Pliny the Elder, once remarked that 'nature excels in its smallest details'. Much of the intricate beauty of nature is lost to us because we are in a hurry and cannot take time to examine closely and patiently. We cast a blind eye even to those species which grow commonly all around us. Take for example, the milkweed.

Because of an opportunistic nature, milkweeds are often looked on as common weeds, good for only children to enjoy blowing the silken seeds into an autumn wind.

Closer examination of the flowers in the round inflorescence reveals a uniquely ornate structure, with the disk-shaped stigma surrounded by five colorful hoods which terminate in hooks. The five sepals are swept back towards the stem, giving the milkweeds a most distinctive look. Many species also exude a delightful fragrance. Another interesting facet of the milkweed is its prevalence at prehistoric Indian sites. Fred Dunford, staff archeologist at the Museum of Natural History in Brewster, states that a majority of the centuries-old midden (shell) heaps left by the Cape's first inhabitants are commonly garbed in a field of milkweed plants. The calcium provided by the old shells might 'sweeten' the soil just enough to establish a milkweed colony.

By far the most beautiful of the milkweeds is butterfly-weed. The blazing orange-red umbels can be seen a long way in its preferred habitat of dry hay-fields and sandplains. Once fairly common in southern New England, the decline of butterfly-weed is related to the demise of agriculture, grazing and fires in the region. It is still common on Martha's Vineyard due to that island's intact fields and meadows.

Its attractiveness has also resulted in over-collection by wild flower fanciers. (A neighbor lucky enough to own land where the wild plants grow often complained to this writer of midnight raiding parties by trowel-wielding members of the local garden club.) Butterfly-weed has a long history as a root medicine, actually being sold in drugstores till the early twentieth century as pleurisy-root. Its medicinal properties are attested to in this passage from a 1907 herbal medicine text; "It is used in disordered digestion and in affections of the lungs, in the last-named instance to promote expectoration, relieve pains in the chest, and induce easier breathing. It is also useful in producing perspiration."

We trust if the reader has a chest cold, that a more standard remedy will be used!

July-August   Dry Fields; Meadows

Butterfly-weed   *Asclepias tuberosa*

Broom Crowberry   *Corema conradii*   Torr.

The habitat of heath and dune presents a challenge to all plant species which grow there. Desiccating, salt-laden wind, a merciless sun and sandy, nutrient-poor soils create a need for rigorous adaptive devices common to many of these plants. Such adaptations include needle-like or waxy leaves, low, sprawling profile and either extensive, shallow root systems or a single, very long taproot.

The harsh environment of the heathland is similar in many respects to that found on mountaintops. In fact, several heath species such as *Hudsonia*, three-toothed cinquefoil and broom crowberry are found in both habitats.

Broom crowberry is a low, evergreen shrub which forms mounds as much as ten feet across. It blooms earliest of any species of the heathland, with hundreds of dark red male flowers shedding pollen in mid-March. A closer look will reveal these staminate flowers to be all stamens and no petals.

Though this plant bears resemblance to other dry habitat species, it is unusual for several reasons. Its range covers the coastal plain from Newfoundland to Cape Cod, then jumps to the New Jersey Pine Barrens and the Shawangunk Mountains of New York. It belongs to a tiny family, the Crowberries, which contains just four species, none closely related to any other plant.

It is quite rare in Massachusetts,though it can be locally abundant on the lower Cape from Wellfleet north and in scattered locations in Plymouth County, (an old name for it was Plymouth Crowberry). Like many sandplain species, this plant has been hurt by loss of habitat through woody succession due to fire suppression, as well as development and recreation pressures. It is listed as a Special Concern species by the state Natural Heritage Program.

The Greek name, *Corema*, means broom, an apt description of the plant's bushy appearance. The derivation of the common name is more obscure, though it's hard to believe that the wily crow would ever have to resort to eating the mealy, tasteless berries.

March-April   Heathlands

78

Broom Crowberry   *Corema conradii*

Blue Curls   *Trichostema dichotomum*   L.

The sandy, dry roadside margins of late August would hardly seem the ideal situation for colorful and fragrant wildflowers. Yet without fail, as summer fades towards Labor Day, the graceful blue curls begins to display itself along the region's highways and gravel aprons.

An attractive and ornate plant, this species' most spectacular feature is four beautifully arched stamens of a violet hue which seem to spring from under the long, upper lip out over the shorter, lower one. This arrangement is reversed slowly as the flower matures into senescence, with the spent stamens ultimately positioned on the bottom. At this point, the pollen-laden anthers no longer need to dust the backs of pollinators once fertilization is accomplished.

Blue curls is entirely covered with fragrant, sticky glands which make it clammy to the touch. Its scent is similar in pungency to a balsam fir. The aromatic quality of this plant has made it popular in the past as a tea and cachet.

The flowers are dark violet with a touch of white mottling inside the corolla. Its exotic scent and square stem makes its membership in the vast Mint Family (*Lamiaceae*) self-evident.

This tough, little annual thrives in inhospitable soils from Maine to North Carolina, but seems most at home along the mid-Atlantic coastal plain. Many plants which colonize such austere habitats are vagabonds from other countries, pinned with the label 'WEED'; blue curls is a true New England native which somehow musters the energy to adorn our unlovely road shoulders with a welcome display of form and fragrance.

August-September   Dry Open Soil

Blue Curls *Trichostema dichotomum*

Sickle-leaved Golden Aster *Chrysopsis falcata* (Purch) Elliot

In the last days of July one of the very first signs that summer's end is nigh can be found along the cinder aprons of railroad tracks and the sterile, dry fields of waste lots. Radiant bursts of sickle-leaved golden aster decorate these otherwise drab habitats.

As with many species which thrive in near-desert conditions, the golden aster grows quickly and forms roundish mounds or colonies no more than a foot high. The falcate or sickle-shaped leaves are covered with a cottony flocculence which helps retard desiccation from sun and salt spray.

This species of golden aster lives strictly along the coastal plain, from New Jersey north to southeastern Massachusetts. While still common, the sickle-leaf's limited range and vulnerability to habitat destruction earn it a place of concern with other native coastal plain species.

This is the only species of yellow aster in our area. In fact, it is more closely related to the goldenrods than the asters and represents a transitional element between the two great Composite sub-families.

August-October   Dry Sandy Fields

Sickle-leaved Golden Aster *Chrysopsis falcata*

Wood Lily   *Lilium philadelphicum*   L.

"Consider the lilies of the field, even Solomon in all his glory was not arrayed like one of these." Matthew 6:28,29

While the famed botanist quoted above was probably referring to the scarlet anemones common in Palestine at the time, the true Lilies have a long and deserved reputation for great beauty and symbolism.

While there are many plants in the Liliaceae family, including onion, garlic, asparagus and trillium, membership in the genus *Lilium* is much more exclusive. This includes only the 'true' lilies which bear one to many, large, six-parted showy flowers at or near the summit of the plant. Among cultivated lilies, the Easter or Madonna lily, *Lilium candidum*, became the emblem of purity, bedecking church altars to honor the Virgin. Once pollinated, this lily reputedly lost its sweet fragrance, changing instead to a foul, fetid odor. This led to much conscientious stamen-plucking by concerned clergymen determined to prevent malodorous fertilization.

Among the wild, native species of lilies, a scant few eke out an existence in southeastern Massachusetts. Arguably the most brilliant is the wood or wild red lily. With flaming orange-red blossoms growing erect on the top of the stem, it is the only wild lily in this region whose flowers gaze at the sky and not the ground. The petals and sepals (or tepals, for you purists) narrow to slender claws which join the ovary below, lending an interesting view through the flower from above. The leaves and stem are an unusual glaucous green color, with the leaves arranged in whorls around the two foot high stem.

Like most of the open field-sandplain species, wood lily is losing ground to both development and successional pressures on its habitat. A few can been seen growing along thin wood edges, where the oak and pitch pine has spread into what was once open pasture. This eventually shades out intolerant species like the lily.

As with many sun-loving species (see bushy rockrose) the best areas left to the wood lily appear to be utility line right-of-ways. Through mechanical and chemical means, the utility companies keep these areas open, providing the sun and lack of competition it needs to flourish and dazzle wandering lily lovers.

July-August   Dry Fields; Thin Wood Edges

Wood Lily   *Lilium philadelphicum*

New England Blazing-star *Liatris scariosa* var. *nova-angliae* Lunell

At first glance this wand of wildflowers looks like a refugee from a western prairie or a kind of horticultural escape. A field of New England blazing-stars, in full flower and waving stiffly in the breeze, does conjure up images of the mid-grass prairies of Kansas and Nebraska, where many species of *Liatris* flourish.

With over thirty-five freely-hybridizing species in North America, New Englanders are fortunate that only one, *Liatris borealis*, occurs here in the Northeast, eliminating identification problems. It is also one of the most impressive of the blazing-stars, standing three feet tall, adorned with 30 to 60 rose-purple flower heads. The leaves are stiffly linear and attached somewhat alternately along the stem. Unbranched and unbowed, the entire aspect of the blazing-star is that of a royal purple scepter.

The New England blazing star is a perennial arising from a roundish corm. It can still occasionally be seen along railroad and utility line right-of-ways in Barnstable County. It is more common on Nantucket, where its native sandplains are still relatively intact.

Don't mistake this regal native of New England for the common, introduced blossoms of the somewhat similar knapweeds. Nondiscriminatory picking, along with woody succession, are both factors in the fairly rapid decline of this open heath species, which simply looks too nice in a vase for its own good.

August-September   Dry Open Heaths; Fields

New England Blazing-star   *Liatris scariosa* var. *nova-angliae*

Saltwater Cordgrass   *Spartina alterniflora*

Salt Marsh

 F OR THE MOST PART, flowering plants have not colonized the open sea. Products of the emergence of terrestrial ecosystems millions of years ago, only a handful of seed plants now live in open salt water (*Zostera*, the eel grass, is a local example.) Few can gain a root-hold on surf pounded beaches. Only where the sea and land join gently, where salt waters mix with fresh and inch slowly over tidally submerged lands, have wildflowers become part of a thriving ocean community — the salt marsh.

On every Cape Cod shore there are old river valleys that empty into the sea. Broadened when glacial meltwaters swelled their drainage streams, these valleys once stood miles inland of the ocean. Evidence, such as mastodon teeth dredged from Georges Bank, indicates that the shore once lay near the present continental shelf. As Ice Age glaciers melted, sea level rose ever higher, drowning these valleys to form today's bays and harbors.

The larger bays developed protective barrier beaches — spits of sand carried into place by long-shore currents, anchored by pioneering plants. These spits formed protected harbors like those at Plymouth and Provincetown or great marsh-ringed lagoons as at Pleasant Bay and Sandy Neck. The higher, more contorted coast of Buzzards Bay encouraged the development of small marshes at the head of every cove and cranny, like those at Back River, Mink Cove, and Little Harbor.

In these tranquil ocean backwaters a dynamic community of plants and animals has developed. In their classic book, *Life and Death of the Salt Marsh,* John and Mildred Teal cite studies that show the salt marsh to be the most productive ecosystem on earth. The biomass

89

production of the salt marsh grasses — the two *Spartina* species and *Distychlis* — is prodigious. Centuries of accumulated growth form deep peats, raising the marsh above the reach of the still rising ocean. Within these salt-washed, mucky prairies a very special sub-set of flowering plants has found a place. Members of a variety of plant families, they share certain evolutionary features such as succulence and salt-resistance.

Salt marshes have never offered much to enterprising humans. In colonial times they were harvested of hay or used as hard-luck pastures. Over the years men have sought to eliminate these areas as pest-breeders; criss-cross drainage ditches mark most of our salt marshes, mute evidence to these efforts. Fortunately, such schemes failed and today the wholesale filling of saltmarshes has been replaced with a new awareness of their many natural values.Those who seek the wildflowers of the salt marsh should do so with great care, in respect to the complex, hidden community on which they intrude.

Represented in the following pages are blossoms both inspiring and inconspicuous, all sharing a salt water birthright. They stand in witness at the spawning grounds and nurseries of many of our most valuable seafood species.

- jw

Sea Lavender

Turk's Cap Lily

Groundsel Tree or Sea Myrtle

Silverweed

Saltmarsh Fleabane

Cat-tail

Seaside Gerardia

Rose Mallow

Sea Lavender   *Limonium carolinianum*   (Walter) Britton

Scattered throughout our coastal salt marshes is a dainty wild-flower reminiscent of the florist's babies breath. Because this plant, known as sea lavender, keeps its pale purple color even after drying, it is a popular addition to dried bouquets. Many a windowsill and shelf top far from the coast are decorated with a nose-gay of sea lavender, reminding its gatherer of the heat, mosquitoes, fragrance, and light that linger over the salt marshes of Cape Cod Bay.

Sole representative of the Leadwort Family among the wild plants of our region, the sea lavender is related to the plants statice and thrift sometimes found in gardens. "Statice," meaning astringent, was once the name of the genus, and the woody base of sea lavender was used for that medicinal purpose. Also known as marsh rosemary, for its sweet fragrance, the present genus name is from the Latin *leimon* meaning "marsh." The plant appears to be conspecific with the southern species *L. carolinianum*. Together, these two varieties spread a lavender haze across salt marshes along the entire Atlantic seaboard, from Texas to Newfoundland. Unfortunately this habitat is limited, vulnerable, and highly desirable for dredging, filling, and development.

An innocent enough pastime, the gathering of sea lavender is no longer recommended. With an increasing influx of tourists and year-round residents salt marshes are losing their special shade of the color purple, and some towns have passed by-laws prohibiting the practice of picking the blooms. There was a time when most natural pursuits on the South Shore and Cape were "innocent enough" — but whether it be beach buggy rides, nude sun-bathing, beach plum gathering, or house building, too much of an innocent thing soon destroys its charm. Like many things in a population-stressed world, the sea lavender bouquet is slipping away, a victim of our own too much, too many, too fast.

July - September   Salt Marsh

92

Sea Lavender   *Limonium carolinianum*

Turk's Cap Lily   *Lilium superbum* L.

Frankly, it is hard to believe that this is a wildflower. So robust and showy that it seems a cultivated garden sport, the Turk's cap lily is in fact a native of the Massachusetts coastal plain, finding its preferred habitat in areas of year-round dampness. Most often on the Cape that means the landward edge of salt marshes, where the groundwater around the plant's big, underground bulbs is mostly fresh. Superlatives are commonplace with this lily. Some individuals can grow to be nearly eight feet tall, and there are records of up to 40 flowers on one ephemeral stalk. And such flowers: bright orange spotted with brown, with 6 swept-back petals that, taken together, have the appearance of a turban. Emerging (or versatile, as the technical manuals say) from the petals are the flower's working parts: six long white stamens tipped with huge brown anthers, and an equally long pistil. 'Improbable' is an apt description of the plant's appearance.

Photographing the Turk's cap lily can be a learning experience. The first impulse is to get the whole bouquet into the picture, but the flowers range all over the top of the whorled, leafy stems. Focusing in on the individual blossoms is even more difficult. They are so long and intricately carved that depth of field is difficult to gauge, and they nod and bounce on the slightest breeze. Besides that, the best-lit blossoms always seem to be on the wettest side of the plant!

Not a true salt marsh dweller, Turk's cap lily often grows at the upper edge of tidally influenced wetlands. In inland situations the observant may find another plant, the tiger lily, an escape from gardens that has become established in damp ditches. The large and even more showy Turk's cap lilies of gardens are a species developed from the Northern European version, *Lilium martagon*. Since nurseries all over the country are creating new and more spectacular varieties of lily for the garden and the Easter dinner table, Turk's cap is best admired in its accustomed place on the edge of our coastal wetlands.

July - September   Edge of salt marsh, wet swales

94

Turk's Cap Lily   *Lilum superbum*

Groundsel Tree or Sea Myrtle   *Baccharis halimifolia*   L.

A glimpse at the scientific name of this plant would make you guess that some intoxicating beverage — suitable to the revelries of the god *Bacchus* — might be derived from this plant. In fact the reason for connecting Bacchus to this plant is lost in the dusty archives of Linnean nomenclature, and those who wish to wet the whistle with groundsel tree wine will be disappointed. An old English name, Consumption-weed, suggests that tuberculosis sufferers might seek a tea of its leaves for rheumatic relief if not a Bacchanalia.

The sea myrtle is one of our plants whose rarity is a product of its geographical range. Few members of the Composite Family in our area are woody shrubs. All of this plant's nearest relatives are denizens of the tropics where the composites, along with most other plant families, gain greater stature. Groundsel tree is equally at home on the Mexican coast, and would probably be happier there when a winter nor'easter strikes the marshes of Cape Cod Bay. On such days the plant will be found, leafless and shaking on the upper marsh border, often in the company of its near relative, the marsh elder. Both plants tolerate the northern climate once established, and are threatened more by the brushcutter clearing a view across the salt marsh than by winter winds.

Unlike most plants in this book the groundsel tree is much more conspicuous in fruit than in bloom. Male and female flowers, drab yellow- green affairs, appear on separate plants, spreading pollen and setting seed with great abandon. The result is a shrub which, suddenly in late summer, appears to have grown white fur. The fur is simply a seed wing called a *pappus* (most familiar as the fuzz of a dandelion's seed.) As in the dandelion, the sea myrtle's pappus serves as a parachute for the seed: a tough little package of life called an *achene*. On close inspection the female shrubs' angled twigs appear to have sprouted countless little shaving-brushes — close packed sets of pappus hairs ready to spread *Baccharis* seeds to cold November winds.

August - September   Border of salt marshes

96

Groundsel Tree or Sea Myrtle   *Baccharis halimifolia*

Silverweed   *Potentilla anserina*   L.

Also called Argentine, another reference to the distinct silvery appearance of the felt-like down on the underside of the leaves. This down is a reminder that a wildflower's lot is not always an easy one. Like skiers and geese (the "anser" of the species name), silverweed finds that down is a splendid insulator against the chill dampness of the shorelines where it sprawls. Growing by reddish runners appressed to the ground, the plant forms colonies on the edge of coastal marshes, lifting up sprightly five-petalled flowers that can carpet an area with splashes of yellow.

There has been some dispute among scientists as to whether the plants which grow on our coast are a different species from those found all across the continent and up to the Arctic Circle. Lately the "lumpers" have prevailed and our species lost the distinction of being our only wildflower named after Hans Egede, the father of modern Greenland.

Being native in Europe as well as North America, silverweed has a long history of herbal use. *Potentilla* means "little powerful one" and was coined in specific reference to this species, not the 121 relatives that grow all over America. Of all its many medicinal uses perhaps Pliny's anti-scrofula concoction is the most imaginative. For this glandular ailment of the young we are instructed to concoct an ointment of crushed silverweed, honey, and axle grease. Chariot axle grease, we assume.

The root of silverweed seems to have been regularly gathered for food by northern peoples. The taste is said to resemble parsnip or sweet potatoes, depending on your taste buds. The *potent* and versatile root also yields an extract which is used to tan leather. Thus we have an amazing little plant which is apothecary, grocery store, chemical factory, and florist shop all in one.

        July - August   Salt marsh borders.

Silverweed *Potentilla anserina*

Saltmarsh Fleabane

Pluchea odorata   (L.) Cass.

Late in the year a low-growing plant hidden among the marsh grasses takes on a pink or purple glow as its brush-like flower heads open to the sultry air.Other members of this group of plants grow far to the south in tropical regions, reminding us that the shores of the Sounds and Buzzards Bay mark a bio-geographic boundary where warm southern waters pile up against the obstruction of southeastern Massachusetts. The result is roses that bloom through November in Woods Hole gardens and a number of southern plants at the "northern limit of range." In New England, *only* here can you commonly see saltmarsh fleabane.

Like many plants which grow in close proximity to the sea or in desert areas, this member of the Aster family is a *succulent*. The best known succulents are cacti, in which the green vegetative parts are thick, fleshy, and often filled with a viscous fluid. This is an adaptation to the dessicating environment of the bone dry desert. But cacti originated in the Carribean, and for seashore plants there is "water, water everywhere and not a drop to drink." Unable to directly use salt water, and apt to lose precious fresh water to salt water by osmosis, the plant adopts a tough skin and swells with a supply of water distilled by metabolic processes for its own needs.

The low, flat-topped flower clusters of *Pluchea* are often dried for flower arrangements, in spite of the other common name, stinkweed. Flower books may tell you that the plant has the odor of camphor — pretty much useless information to modern folk who've lost touch with the herbal basis of our nostrums. Camphor, a sticky, flammable substance obtained from an Oriental evergreen, has been used in moth balls and stimulants for years. Thus, the reputation of this plant as a flea "bane" is based on its resemblance to our common field fleabanes and its faint odor of camphor, a tried and true insect repellent.

September   Salt marsh

Saltmarsh Fleabane   *Pluchea odorata*

101

Cat-tail   *Typha* spp.

Some people might find cat-tail a poor excuse for a wildflower. One botanical text says that the plant is "destitute of a proper floral envelope" another that it has "flowers indefinite", while still another points out that its "petals are merely hairlike bristles". Nonetheless, cat-tails are one of the most conspicuous and ultimately interesting plants of coastal marshes. The club-like portion of the plant, which children love to break off and use as a bat or sword, is the flower wand. The male flowers at the top are a thin yellow candle wick, while the female flowers become the brown, felt-covered sausage that we immediately recognize as a cat-tail.

There are three species of cat-tail in our area, out of four that grow in the U. S. and eighteen worldwide. The cat-tail is a good lesson in how scientists separate plants into like kinds called 'species', groups of plants that breed true and remain identifiable in the wild. Most common in our area is *Typha latifolia* in which the male and female flowers grow in a continuous spike. In other words, the wick and the sausage are connected. If, on the other hand, they are separated by a length of bare green stalk, then the species is either *Typha angustifolia* or *Typha glauca*. How to tell these two apart? Simple enough: *angustifolia* only grows to be 5 feet tall; *glauca* grows six to ten feet tall. These last two are much less common than the first and are more likely to be found at the edge of a coastal marsh where the soil is less acidic.

The details of plant identification are, fortunately, only one aspect of botany. Wild food gatherers have called cat-tails the 'supermarket of the swamps'. Among other uses one can obtain a cooked vegetable (somewhat like corn on the cob) from the young flower spikes, pancakes from flour mixed with the pollen, root sprouts served as salad toppers, root stalks cooked as a starchy side dish, and the white growing tips eaten cooked or raw as 'Cossack asparagus.'

Fortunately for muskrats, blackbirds, and rails, cat-tails have not become popular enough to be exploited. Still, disturbance about the edges of marshes encourages the giant reed to the detriment of many cat-tail stands, thus substituting a sterile monoculture for a plant which, in all its varieties and uses, symbolizes diversity.

June - July   Marshes, wet ditches

Broad-leaved Cat-tail   *Typha latifolia*

Seaside Gerardia   *Agalinis maritima*   Raf.

This plant is one of a number of inconspicuous members of the Foxglove family that inhabit a variety of environments in our region. Their ability to grow in almost every habitat from wooded swamps to dry sandplains to salt-crusted mudflats, make the gerardias a case history in adaptation. Small changes in the plants' structure have led to strains that meet the very rigid demands of these diverse communities. The succulence of seaside gerardia, along with its sprawling growth, deep rhizomous root system, and pale floral color are all single adaptations to the saltmarsh. Taken together they are the makings of a new species, unable to cross-breed with other gerardias. There in a nutshell you have the mechanism of evolution and change.

The flowers of seaside gerardia are formed of 5 petals fused into a tubular form, like flaring trumpets. Since the petal lobes are not equally formed the flower is said to be bilaterally symmetrical. Put more simply, if the flower were divided down the middle each side would be the mirror image of the other. (People are also bilaterally symmetrical — roses and starfish have a five-parted, radial symmetry.) All members of the genus *Agalinis* have rose-purple flowers. Some experts also place the yellow false foxgloves in this genus, others lump them together in the genus *Gerardia*, while still others classify the yellow forms in genus *Aureolaria*. Evolution and change are equally active in the world of plant taxonomy.

Seaside gerardia is closely tied to the salt marsh, and it shares the same environmental dilemmas. Plants in salty surroundings, where there is regular flooding, were not made for the pressure of grazing animals or other hard use. The popularity of the salt marsh for walking, especially on the drier landward edges, subjects this plant to trampling. Filling of marsh edges to get "just one more" building lot or front yard has also been hard on seaside gerardia. New laws prevent such activities without reconstruction efforts, but the fragile nature of gerardia makes it a doubtful transplant to a man-made marsh.

August - September   Saltmarsh

Seaside Gerardia *Agalinis maritima*

Rose Mallow
Hibiscus moscheutos L.

Imagine yourself slogging through an impenetrable marsh, sometimes falling to your knees in tepid water or a clinging muck. Machete in hand, you hack your way through tall reeds, tangled vines, thorny brush, all rising over your head and blocking out the burning sun. Suddenly you stop and there before your eyes is a bower of gigantic hibiscus flowers, each blossom big as your outstretched hand, some with pink petals, others white with cherry red centers, all with yellow central columns that stick out at you like the tongue of so many snakes.

This description may sound like something out of the Amazon jungles. But this is an experience you might have in the Barnstable Great Marshes or along the overgrown edges of many a tidal marsh in our area. In size and proportion this is probably our most unlikely wildflower, a prize worth the summer heat and biting flies that often accompany its discovery.

The connection of hibiscus to the South is not surprising — few members of this family grow north of Massachusetts. Though quite celebrated (its blossom graces the cover of more than one wildflower guide) the rose mallow is not as well known as some of its relatives. Its other common names hint at these connections: "wild cotton" is a reminder that cultivated cotton is in this family; "sea hollyhock" conjures up visions of the garden relative; and "marsh mallow" is a reference to the true marsh-mallow plant from which a sticky paste (common to all members of the family) was once extracted to make marshmallows. A final link to the South involves the relative okra, whose mucilaginous juices add consistency to gumbos.

So the rose mallow keeps good company in the plant world — and keeps to its own special places in our salt marshes, never common and not meant for picking, as the blossoms quickly fade and have a "mousey" smell. If your curiosity is piqued by what a "mousey" smell might be, put on your slogging sneakers and make for the high salt marsh in August. The sight of the flowers, at least, will be worth the effort.

August - September   Brackish marshes

106

Rose Mallow *Hibiscus moscheutos*

Dunes and Beaches

WHITE HORSE BEACH, Clark's Island, Onset Beach, Sandy Neck, South Cape Beach, the Provincelands, Old Silver Beach. The names invoke a hundred pleasant summer memories for visitors — and remind those who live here of silent winter days or raging nor'easters. The one overwhelming impression of that stretch of land from Duxbury to P-Town, from Marion to Chatham, which we loosely call "the Cape", is one of *SAND*. Sand in your lunch, sand in your hair, sand in your walkman, and, mostly, sand in your shoes. The feel of it is enough to carry you back to that salt air, that warm breeze, that special kind of light, that memory that means "Cape Cod."

Despite this human romanticism about dunes and beaches, sand is our least hospitable wildflower habitat. The flowers which manage to grow on dunes and beaches must be adapted to conditions like those of the desert. Since trees cannot survive here, there is no shade, no respite from the relentless ultraviolet rays of the sun. The unbroken terrain is swept by almost constant winds, sometimes moist with storm mists, but usually dessicating and salt-laden. At the ocean's edge, fresh water is scarce. Most of the region's 40 inches of rainfall seeps quickly through the sand and is lost to all but the most deeply rooted plants. Finally, there is the sand itself, devoid of nutrients, constantly on the move, threatening to overpower any plant that hasn't evolved a mechanism to avoid being buried alive.

Some of these adaptations are discussed in the following section which deals with practically all of the conspicuous flowers of the shifting sands — a very small number of species. These species share their domain with our most remarkable dune plant, *Ammophila breviligulata*, the American beachgrass. You'd think the word adaptable was invented to describe this versatile native grass that can take root on the most barren dune. Sending yards and yards of underground runners through the sand, raising its flower heads above a swiftly growing dune, setting a huge supply of seed to ripen like golden grain in the mellow coastal autumn: this plant is the epitome of survival on sand. Conservationists who've spent back-breaking hours pushing tufts of beachgrass into the sand in desperate efforts to stabilize a dune ridge know that *Ammophila* is the savior of our coastline.

Conflicts between recreational use of dunes and wild plants' struggle for survival have too often been settled in our favor. The result has been anything but favorable to any of us. Dunes and barrier beaches guard the inhabited coastline from storm surges. The hundreds of sun bathers who blissfully stalk the back dunes of Plymouth Beach are trampling our best coastal defense system. The dune-buggy enthusiasts who insist on accesss to the beaches and dunes of the Outer Cape ignore the fragility of this ecosystem. The dunes and beaches of Cape Cod and Buzzards Bays, of Nantucket and Vinyard Sounds, are a backyard for millions, where humans meet the sea on friendly terms. But those same beaches and dunes must face the sea on stormy terms. When those times come the dunelands must be healthy, intact, stabilized by a cover of very specialized and very sensitive plants. The sooner we learn to walk softly there, the better for us all.

— jw

Sea Rocket

Beach Plum

Salt-spray Rose

Dusty Miller

Beach Pea

Seaside Goldenrod

Sea Rocket

Cakile edentula   (Bigel.) Hook.

In his 1887 *Flora* the pioneer American botanist Asa Gray, in his customary spare language, characterizes this plant as "wild on the shore of the sea and Great Lakes." Although later scientists determined that much of the inland population is a different variety, his words still ring true to the beach comber who finds this plant sprawled along the base of dunes or bluffs, just out of reach of summer tides. Here, above a buried line of decaying vegetation deposited by winter storm tides, there are just enough nutrients in the beach sand to nourish plants like sea rocket that grow "wild on the shore."

Member of the Mustard family, the sea rocket's relatives are widespread food and forage crops. Like its cousin the horseradish, sea rocket's young shoots have a pleasantly hot taste and their fleshy, succulent nature makes them a good salad garnish. Most mustards — or *crucifers* as they were once called, in reference to their four-petalled, cross-shaped flowers — are best recognized by their seed pods, long and pointed and looking much like Chinese rockets (accounting for the seemingly modern name which is really quite antique). Sea rocket's missiles are stubby, with two seeds inside the bean-like fruit (the silique).

Sea rocket's small, pale lavender blossoms can be looked for anytime from July into late November. At home in the sands of both Buzzards and Cape Cod Bays, this plant takes advantage of the moderate nature of the beach climate, enjoying the warmth retained by sea water through the winter months. Although this plant is known to grow along sandy beaches in Iceland and the Azores, it is replaced in Europe by *Cakile maritima*. Beach combers interested in adding to the scientific knowledge of our shores might look for this European import here. Told by its deeply toothed leaves, this plant has not yet been reported from Cape Cod. Finding it might not make you famous, but that's not what beach combing's about.

July - November   Beaches

112

Sea Rocket   *Cakile edentula*

Beach Plum   *Prunus maritima*   Marsh.

A staple of the Cape Cod breakfast table, beach plum jelly has a flavor distilled from salt wind and sandy soil. To savor this delight you need only step into any gift shop on a Cape backroad or along Plymouth's waterfront. There, amid imported knick-knacks, one can usually find a precious jar filled with the purple essence of this native fruit. Better not read the fine print, for the beach plum grows from Deleware to Maine and your Cape Cod souvenir may have been cooked up at a mass-production plant in New Jersey. To avoid this pitfall, head for the dunes with sun hat on head and collecting basket in arm. Many wild foods cook books have jelly recipes. The smell of the bubbling jam from your kitchen stove will bring back memories of the ocean air.

The plums, miniature versions of the orchard's Damsons and just as lucious, are far easier to pick. The plant's sprawling habit is a derivation of the growth form of many fruiting trees, suited to the sterile and gale-swept dunes on which it grows. The fruits of members of the genus *Prunus* are called 'drupes', but you know them better as plums, cherries, apricots, and peaches. All share the fleshy outer coating — so tempting to animals and humans — and a hard inner seed cover, the pit. This cover protects the seed as it passes through the digestive system, so that birds and other animals often plant seeds with their droppings (which serve as a ready-made fertilizer.) Not all *Prunus* pits are casually thrown aside — the mythical anti-cancer drug laetrile is made from apricot pits, and the almond is a member of this family.

Beach plum has a long history of use as food; the local Wampanoag Indians used it as an ingredient in pemmican long before Pilgrim gardeners cultivated cuttings in their cottage gardens. Spectacular in bloom, the plant seems most at home in those wild dunelands where it originated.

May - June   Dunes, roadsides

114

Beach Plum   *Prunus maritima*

Salt-spray Rose

Rosa rugosa   Thunb.

Many of the flowers found in this book require the intervention of scientists or plant societies to prevent careless destruction of their habitats. But in this case turnabout is fair play. A fine example of a truly naturalized plant, this Asian import has come to the aid of conservationists as a protector of barrier beaches.

Cape legend had it that *Rosa rugosa* arrived on these shores after the wreck of the *Franklin,* a ship carrying botanical specimens from the Far East in 1849. This has since been disproved, as the first appearance of this showy rose was in the 1870s. No doubt the plant was introduced more than once along the coast, for it has the uncanny ability to produce great bushy masses of greenery topped by red and white blossoms from a soil that is little more than loose sand. Spreading and sprawling, its six-foot branches covered with spines, the plant is a formidable barrier that deters trampling feet and anchors wandering dunes, those natural defenders of our coastline.

'Naturalized' species are those which are brought into an area and take a firm hold, establishing themselves as a part of the natural vegetative community. As fond of roadsides as of dunes, salt-spray rose seems a vital part of the Cape landscape, and has indeed served a useful purpose, replacing plants which could not tolerate the abuse of pedestrian traffic. (Not all naturalized species are so welcome, see the introduction to the following section.)

One reason for this rose's success is the prominence of its hips. Hips are the fleshy fruits of roses, a favored wildlife food leading, by process of animal elimination, to the spread of seed along our shores. Ounce for ounce, rose hips contain more Vitamin C than oranges. Although this was well known during World War II, when rose hip tablets were used to prevent scurvy, their popularity has boomed in recent years thanks to Dr.Pauling's reputed preventative of the common cold. Salt-spray rose hips are prized for jellies and jams, and we encourage their use to supplement the native and less common beach plum.

June - October   Dunes and roadsides

Salt-spray Rose *Rosa rugosa*

Dusty Miller
Artemisia stelleriana Bess.

Walk across low dunes, or the grassy areas just above high tide line on any of our beaches, and you are likely to see a mass of greyish stems and leaves sprawled across the ground. Colonizing by underground runners just as beach grass does, dusty miller seems a natural inhabitant of our coastal sands. But, if you brush the dust from a nineteenth century botany text and turn to *Artemisia* you will not find the species *stelleriana*. Up until 1880 or so this plant was confined to gardens. Some circumstance — perhaps only a fad among gardeners — led to its escape to wild surroundings where it flourished as a component of our sand-anchoring flora.

A member of the Aster family, dusty miller is not known for its flowers. The clusters of hermaphroditic, tubular blossoms are of a yellowish-green color that blends with the surrounding vegetation. The plant is noticed for its unusual hoary appearance, the leaves being a subtle shade of mixed gray, white and green. In gardens the plants are cultivated for their aromatic properties, though wild populations seem to have lost this trait. Both of these characteristics lead back to the derivation of its antique common and classical scientific names.

Grist mills are no longer neighborhood institutions, but in the days when you made regular trips to the mill they were common along the small streams of southeastern Massachusetts. Turned by a wooden water wheel, the grindstones converted corn and wheat to meal and flower. The proprietor of the mill always wore a film of flour over his regular clothes, giving him the frosted look of a *dusty miller*. Thus, this plant.

The aromatic quality of plants in this group — including wormwood and sage — accounts for their use in incense and funeral balms, making the connection to Artemisia, the wife of King Mausolus. This fellow was best known for his tomb, a wonder of the ancient world called the Mausoleum, a word that is now generic for any above-ground crypt. Thus, you have the making of a clasical education as you stroll over the dunes to the beach.

May - September   Dunes, beaches

Dusty Miller   *Artemisia stelleriana*

Beach Pea

Lathyrus maritimus
(Ser.) Eames

No flowering, rooted plant can survive on the open beach within reach of the surf, but beach pea comes close, trailing fleshy vines to the very edge of the tide line. There it shares the shore with sand and salt tolerant species from other families — clotbur from the Asters, sea milkwort from the Primroses, and *Ammophila*, the hardy beach Grass. Each of these has its own way of dealing with the harsh conditions at the edge of the land, but the magenta flowers of Beach Pea make it the easiest to admire.

Belonging to a genus which includes the garden sweet pea, vetchling (a marsh species,) and the everlasting pea (a plant that's overrun many an abandoned garden around old Cape homesteads), the beach pea is truly "cosmopolitan". In a botanical sense this means that it is native to many areas of the world. Places as diverse as Greenland, Labrador, the Great Lakes, Oregon, Japan, and Chile all have their own geographic race of beach pea. All share the vine growth form, all have angled branches and leaves tipped with a clasping tendril, all have distinctive arrow-shaped stipules at the base of each leaf.

Because of its size (3/4 of an inch or better) the beach pea is an ideal study of the unique shape of a pea flower. The two lower petals unite to form a *keel*, the two side petals form *wings*, and the top petal is held aloft as the *standard*. These flowers give way in late summer to flattened pea pods, crisp and edible when young, but often infested with green worms as they age.

According to legend, the scientific name derives from the Greek "la thuros" meaning "very passionate", an allusion to aphrodisiac properties. Although we make no claims for the properties of beach pea, it is documented that these plants have been witness to many "la thuros" moments on Cape Cod beaches.

May - July   Dunes and shores

120

Beach Pea   *Lathyrus maritimus*

Seaside Goldenrod   *Solidago sempervirens*   L.

Asa Gray called the goldenrods "characteristic plants of the American autumn." Overrunning roadsides and fallow grounds in bewildering numbers and varieties, they are *the* strain of native plants best adapted to open ground. Still, for all their success, goldenrods have an undeserved reputation for plaguing hay fever sufferers. Fact is, goldenrod pollen is much too heavy to reach our nostrils through the air. The misery is caused by the pollen of ragweed, an inconspicuous plant that blooms at the same time as goldenrod. The English, who've far fewer species and much more respect for the plant, take note of the melancholy in goldenrod yellow and call the plant "farewell summer."

Solidago sempervirens (meaning "evergreen healing plant") is the most robust of the lot, despite its favored habitat at the cutting edge of the sea. While most goldenrod flowers are too small to be noticeable except *en masse*, the individual flowers of this species are prominent. A close look reveals the ray and disk flowers that mark this as a relative of the asters. The long, fleshy basal leaves, visible early in the season, give rise to late summer flower stalks that may reach eight feet. Often the weight of the flowers bends these stalks toward the ground. Blooming through November in good years, the tall brown stem topped with fuzzy seeds is a familiar silhouette on the winter skyline of the dunes.

Seaside goldenrod requires sites in close proximity to the ocean — beaches, dunes, and roadsides on the immediate coast. Although the plant is holding its own where these habitats are undisturbed, evolution is at work within the goldenrod group. This species frequently hybridizes with *Solidago rugosa*, our most common thicket-forming goldenrod. So where these plants meet at the upper edge of tide water, nature is providing a vector for the movement of seaside goldenrod genes to higher ground.

September - November   Beaches, dunes, salt marsh

Seaside Goldenrod   *Solidago sempervirens*

Alien Species

PLANTS HAVE ADAPTED to all of the earth's environments, and each species has worked out its own method of dispersal. Seeds come in a variety of shapes and sizes, but share the single purpose of colonizing new areas. Maple "keys" fly though the air like whirling helicopter blades, dandelion and cottonwood seeds float on gossamer parachutes, burdocks stick to pants legs and animal fur, cherry seeds pass unscathed through the intestinal tract of birds, enormous coconuts float across the world's oceans, and orchid seeds as fine as dust are carried vast distances by the wind.

In New England the most prodigious feats of spreading seed were aided by that relative latecomer, the European immigrant. In grain sacks, in garden seed packets, in worn satchels and shoes, came the seeds of plants that shared the settlers' Old World fields. The pernicious weed plantain is such an immediate follower of European colonists that it is called "white man's foot", springing up wherever he steps.

Many alien plants, whether of European or Asian origin (few African or South American plants can stand the New England climate), have become well known and appreciated components of our flora. Our wealth of roadside flowers would be impoverished were it not for those flowers, suited to disturbed sites, which the settlers brought to these shores. New England's native plants were suited to forest communities. Only a few lived in rich, grassy glades along river bottoms or on dry ridges. In such intervals the Indians set fires to retard the growth of trees.

The new environments created by settlers were gardens, fields, pastures: inhospitable to trout lilies, bunchberry, and lady-slipper. These woodland plants retreated before the plow, surviving in remnant woodlots and returning as settlement proceeded west and forests returned. In sunny, grass-dominated roadsides and fields the foreigners — dandelion, buttercup, daisy, devil's paintbrush — found a place.

Unfortunately, too many introduced species of plants are opportunists which can capitalize on a variety of environments, including the last strongholds of our natives. The resemblance to White/Indian history is painfully apt: there is good reason for calling wildflower preserves "reservations." The honeysuckles are a good example of this floral counterpart to Manifest Destiny. Both the shrubby Morrow's honeysuckle and the Japanese vine are non-native plants which have crowded out the original vegetation. Accidental or planned, introductions can go awry. Such was the case in Florida where the beautiful water hyacinth is a major pest, clogging waterways and choking aquatic systems. The competive advantage, however slight, can make the alien a nightmare worthy of a science fiction thriller.

Here we choose to spotlight a group of more benign immigrants — plants new to Plymouth and Barnstable Counties that have yet to become firmly established. Some are held in check by our climate, some have very restrictive habitat requirements, some are simply so new that they've yet to travel far from their original port of arrival. In common with the many native plants discussed here, they are unusual, rare, or eye-catching and can serve as indicators of the health of our regional environment. All, for the moment, are welcome additions to our floral melting pot or, more accurately, our floral mosaic.

— jw

Yellow Iris

Sea Poppy

Sheep's Bit

Trumpet Creeper

Scotch Broom

Lance-leaf Coreopsis

Yellow Iris   *Iris pseudacorus*   L.

Wild European plants have been 'tamed' in much the same way we think of animals being domesticated. Many of these flowers come to depend on cultivation and scarcely persist once a garden is abandoned, failing in competition with introduced weeds or native vegetation. Still, plants do wander from gardens. In the 1800's it was noted that yellow iris was now "sometimes spontaneous," indicating that its seeds had found their way by natural methods to its favored habitat. Today the plant is widely established in New England wetlands, where it adds to our early summer blossom show without becoming an overbearing 'weed.'

Yellow iris, or yellow flag, is native to the marshes of England and northern Europe. In France it was the original "Flower of Louis", named for that country's kings and still with us today as the "fleur-de-lis" of banners and decorative seals. The flower parts are unique: colored sepals spread downward as "falls" and the petals arch upward as "standards".

Planted in the shallows of ornamental pools in Victorian gardens, the yellow iris is perrenial and easy to maintain as long as it has wet roots. Spreading by thick pink-fleshed rhizomes, buried in rich marsh muck, the plant forms clumps of spear shaped leaves among which the brilliant yellow flowers appear. Iris rhizomes have a variety of uses — a perfume ingredient called "essence of violets" is derived from some; this species yields a black dye used in the manufacture of ink. The modern imagination probably cannot fathom the curiosity which led some ancient herbalist to dig up iris roots for fun and profit.

A colony of yellow iris, mingled with the native rose mallow, has bloomed for many years in a brackish marsh adjacent to Route 6-A in Sandwich. In recent years the invasive *Phragmites* grass, encouraged by human disturbance, has begun to crowd out these flowers. Thus, our wild areas are often the products of centuries of disturbance, by gardener's trowel or dredger's power shovel.

June - July   Marshes and brooksides

Yellow Iris *Iris pseudacorus*

Sea Poppy   *Glaucium flavum*   Crantz

This wildflower might well be called a *waif*, a European import which exists tenuously in only two or three locations on the shores of Buzzards Bay and Nantucket Sound. Once found, the unmistakeable yellow blossoms will bring the botanist back year after year.

Known primarily from coastal strands where it grows in seemingly inhospitable gravel piles and stretches of open sand, the sea poppy seems reluctant to bid farewell to the ocean which its seeds so recently crossed. A few years ago a colony was found at the tip of Stony Point Dike in Wareham. This man-made peninsula protecting the Cape Cod Canal is the only known Plymouth County location for this species, accessible to the public only by boat. The plant has become established elsewhere on the Eastern seaboard, and is still raised in gardens, often in a delicate orange-flowered variety.

The sea poppy has a number of characters which make it an interesting botanical find. The huge rosette of deeply cut, hoary leaves is especially conspicuous in the sparsely vegetated areas where it sprouts. In early summer a tall flower stalk rises from these leaves, topped by solitary, four-petalled yellow blossoms. The most intriguing aspect of the plant is the seed capsule which develops from the flower: a pencil-thin, curving affair up to 12 inches long which has led some to call this the "horn poppy." Those who pick the flower or its seed pod will quickly discover that sea poppy, in common with many members of this family, has a viscous, colored sap which is annoying to those with sensitive skin.

May - June   Coastal sand and gravel banks

Sea Poppy *Glaucium flavum*

131

Sheep's Bit   *Jasione montana*   L.

Don't look for this flower in most popular field guides (an exception is Venning's *Wildflowers of North America*, where the drawing bears little resemblance to the real thing). Sheep's bit is a recent and little-noticed addition to America's flora, with a range limited to local pockets of growth scattered from New Jersey to Massachusetts.

A common field plant in Europe (where the ancient healer Theophrastus named it after *iasis*, the Greek word for healing), this delicate blue flower is only now coming into its own in our area. In Plymouth County it is expanding outward from a center in the Wareham - Middleboro - New Bedford triangle; on Cape Cod it is following roadsides and suburban lawns outward from the Marstons Mills - East Sandwich area.

A Bluebell family member, sheep's bit bears little resemblance to its larger relatives. In fact, at a distance the linear-leaved plant most closely resembles a thistle or knapweed. The tiny flowers gather in a tight hemispherical cluster at the top of thin stalks, each cornflower blue blossom revealing its bluebell character only on close inspection.

Although there are currently no sheep along the edge of I-495, the mowing bars of the Massachusetts DPW keep the grass at a height comparable to that of the European pastures where sheep's bit is at home. In time we may very well dismiss this plant as just another weed, like dandelions and clovers, but for now it holds a special place in our regional environment as a recent immigrant that seems to have found a niche here.

July - August   Roadsides and lawns

Sheep's Bit *Jasione montana*

Trumpet Creeper   *Campsis radicans*   (L.) Seem.

With careful cultivation, aided by a recent moderation in climate, plants from the American South have become established in our region. All of Cape Cod, as well as those portions of Plymouth County along the immediate coast, are in the most tolerant of New England's climatic zones and it's no secret that some representatives of tropical families can thrive here. Trumpet creeper vine and the catalpa tree are our only representatives of the Bignonia family, an important component of South American rain forests.

Trumpet creeper has been encouraged in gardens not only for its ease of cultivation, but for its trumpet-shaped flowers, 2 1/2 to 3 inches long. A favorite of hummingbirds, the flowers are soaked with a sticky-sweet nectar that also makes them irresistable to ants — a consideration when planting near the home. A mass of creeper climbing a trellis can be a memorable sight when at the height of its bloom, or when the flower capsules swell into six-inch long curved seed pods.

But the same qualities which recommend trumpet creeper to the gardener may not be desirable in the wild. Any plant described as "a vigorous climber" or "handsome in cultivation but becoming an aggresive weed" must be held suspect. As a woody vine which sets out aerial rootlets on any convenient upright surface, the creeper tends to overwhelm an area, eventually smothering and shading out the vegetation below it. While a vine bower may be fine when held in check by the gardener's shears, nature hasn't that option.

Fortunately for our native vegetation, trumpet creeper (also known by the less appealing name of "cow itch") is held in check by winter freezes and so occupies only a small and inoffensive position in our plant community. One unforeseen consequence of a global warming trend might be an expansion of the stranglehold of trumpet creeper and similar exotic species.

July - August   Banks, woods, roadsides

134

Trumpet Creeper *Campsis radicans*

Scotch Broom   *Cytisus scoparius*   (L.) Link

Consider for a moment the kind of environments we create. Beyond the well-manicured order of yards, gardens, and city parks there are thousands of acres of roadsides, abandoned fields, dumps, and excavation scars left to be colonized by plants. All of these areas have lost their top soil, the legacy of thousands of years of nutrient cycling. None of these areas provides fertile ground for the return of native plants. To remedy this we have imported plants familiar to New England's English founders — plants like the scotch broom, which were known to grow on impoverished soil.

All members of the Pea family obtain vital nitrogen compounds from bacteria which live within their roots. This explains their ability to grow in areas that other plants find intolerable. This competitive advantage has made the scotch broom an unusual but not uncommon sight in coastal New England.

Through much of the year broom has an appearance of dormancy. The vertical branchlets are evergreen and thin enough to look like the needles of some exotic conifer. But in late Spring the branches sprout leaves — many in clover-like triplets — and yellow flowers that soon cover the plant in a glorious, if transient, display. At blossom time bees alighting on the flowers receive a surprise as they land. The weight of the bee releases the style and stamens from their resting place in the flower's keel, and the insect is dusted and probed for pollen before finding its nectar reward.

Soon after flowering the plant takes on its old appearance again, but the flower show is memorable enough to make this a popular garden plant — in several color forms. As a successful transplant in an unpromising situation, scotch broom has become a familiar part of the Cape Cod landscape.

May - June   Roadsides, waste ground

136

Scotch Broom *Cytisus scoparius*

137

Lance-leaf Coreopsis   *Coreopsis lanceolata*   L.

Tourists who visit Cape Cod are sometimes overheard remarking on the beauty of the "yellow daisies" growing on roadsides. Although these flowers might be mistaken for native plants, they are only as natural here as the bulldozed and seeded banks they inhabit. The lance-leaf coreopsis hasn't got a name a tourist could love. But amateur botanists should be happy to be spared the pains of identifying the scores of similar plants which grow wild to our south and west. In fact Western naturalists, despairing of the task, sometimes resort to calling all of them CYC's — 'confusing yellow composites.'

Lance-leaf coreopsis remains a popular garden plant, although it has been widely supplanted by gaudier, two-tone species. Its habit of spreading by stems budded at the base of the plant and its liking for open, disturbed, and sun-drenched ground (similar to its native prairies) make it a welcome resident in this part of the country.

The name coreopsis is from the Greek for "appearing like a bug" and has come to us in English as 'tickseed'. Both names refer to the appearance of the seed, which looks like a small beetle with fangs. The "fangs" are, in fact, fine hooks which help the seed attach to the nearest bird or beast for quick transport to a new location.

One of our most sprightly and cheering flowers in appearance, the coreopsis provides blossom-blanketed meadows where otherwise only grass would grow. As a new addition to our list of wildflowers it is a symbol that the plant communities of the Cape remain vital and dynamic.

        June - July   Roadsides and fields

Lance-leaf Coreopsis *Coreopsis lanceolata*

Plymouth Gentian

Living on the Edge:
Rare & Threatened Wildflowers

THERE ARE ABOUT 2700 plant species, native and introduced, in Massachusetts. Less than 10 percent, 242 species, are officially listed by the Massachusetts Natural Heritage and Endangered Species Program (MNHESP) on the state rare list. Of these 'plants on the edge' 52 are found in Barnstable County.

Since 1978, the MNHESP has documented and compiled the first comprehensive listing of state endangered plants and animals, giving botanists and biologists a clearer picture of current population numbers, trends and potential impacts on vulnerable habitats. Every species station is logged into a computer data base, which includes a strictly confidential mapping system pinpointing the exact location of each taxon. Land planners, municipal regulatory officials, conservation commissions and others have been the recipients of the valuable information garnered by MNHESP.

What causes rarity in a species? In a nutshell, habitat alteration. There are many reasons why changes in habitat occur. Some are caused by nature, but the majority of ecological changes are generally human-induced.

When encroaching oaks and pitch pine threaten to shade out sandplain species like wild lupine or broom crowberry, it is a result of development eradicating fire and grazing as maintainers of open space. When condo development unleashes the effluent from three or four hundred septic systems into the Cape's sandy soil near a coastal plain kettle pond, eutrophication from nutrient loading may impact on the Plymouth gentian or terete arrowhead.

The lure of recreation that these pristine ponds attract lead to beaches, boats, docks and ORV's, which could doom the redroot or New England boneset.

Despite popular misconception, there is no state Endangered Species Act giving legal protection to rare plants or animals in Massachusetts. There are a mere two plant species in the state actually covered by the federal Endangered Species Act (only one, sandplain gerardia, exists on Cape Cod), and even under the ESA, protection is marginal at best.

What to do when faced with a potential threat to a state listed plant? There are several options, but first ask the question - has the plant been positively identified as a rare species? There are several good, non-technical field guides, of which a personal favorite is *Newcomb's Wildflower Guide* by Lawrence Newcomb. Unfortunately, many rare species are simply not common enough for inclusion in popular manuals. This means either ploughing through one of the technical manuals like *Gray's Manual of Botany* by M.L. Fernald, an arduous task even for the experienced field botanist, or seeking help from an expert.

The Massachusetts Natural Heritage and Endangered Species Program is the first place to turn if one is reasonably certain that a rarity is threatened. Obtain as much information as is possible in the field, such as number of plants, general health of the population, approximate per cent in flower, bud, seed and any known threats to the plants. Plot the exact location onto a USGS quad map. Take photos of the plants if possible. The information should be sent to MNHESP, Division of Fisheries and Wildlife, Route 135, Westborough, Massachusetts 01581.

Some species, such as the fringed polygala in Bourne, are regionally significant but are not rare on a state-wide basis. In these cases, local sources of help may need to be explored, such as the town conservation commission, garden club or natural history museum.

If a rare plant is about to be wiped out by development, a sincere appeal to the contractor can lead to surprising success if you are willing to do the footwork. When it looks as though the bulldozer driver could care less, a sympathetic reporter from the local newspaper can create significant pressure on the development company, which derives profits from good public relations.

For those private landowners who know they have rare plants on their property and are unsure of how to protect them, the Nature Conservancy offers a registry program designed to assist the property owner in caring for their prize species.

For transplanting or propagating information, the New England Wildflower Society's Garden in the Woods in Framingham is the logical source to try. The Center for Plant Propagation and Harvard University's Arnold Arboretum, both in Jamaica Plain, Massachusetts can also answer these questions.

The preservation of biological diversity on this planet is the cornerstone of a philosophy which simply states that every species of plant and animal is a vital facet in the warp and woof of existence. To eliminate just one piece is to tear away a little more from the fabric of life.

— mjd

Bushy Rockrose

Bog Candles

Swamp Pink

Golden Club

Fringed Polygala

New England Thoroughwort

Plymouth Gentian

Sandplain Gerardia

Tinker's Weed

Bushy Rockrose   *Helianthemum dumosum (Bickn.)*   Fern.

Bushy rockrose is one of the very few plant species found in our area to have been under review by the U.S. Fish and Wildlife Service for protection under the federal Endangered Species Act. A mere five species in all of New England are currently protected by the Federal Government under this act.

Because it is now documented in forty-nine stations along the coastal plain from Cape Cod to Long Island, New York, federal authorities have for the time being deferred nationally endangered status for bushy rockrose. It is however, listed as a species of Special Concern by the Massachusetts Natural Heritage and Endangered Species Program.

The relatively high number of sightings for this plant is deceiving. All but fifteen locations occur in Barnstable, Dukes and Nantucket counties, making it one of a handful of endemics to the southeastern Massachusetts area. Clearly, the future survival of bushy rockrose depends on its fate in these three counties, (a recent sighting in south Plymouth County represents an isolated northern outlier of its range).

Bushy rockrose was probably much more common when the open moors and sandplains were still unencumbered by the encroaching pitch pines and oaks which now threaten to shade out many of our heathland plants.

Even today, if one knows where to look, this sprawling plant can be found in impressive numbers, with colonies forming mounds of multiple-stemmed plants. Unlike other members of the *Helianthemum* genus (see frostweed in the Sandplains section), bushy rockrose lacks a single main stem or axis. Instead, many diverging branchlets bear five-petalled, lemon yellow flowers. Self-fertilizing cleistogamous flowers found in the leaf axils are not as common in this species as in related species within the Rockrose group.

Close inspection of the leaves and stem reveals another singular characteristic of bushy rockrose; reddish glandular hairs intermixed with star-shaped (stellate) hairs, forming an almost silvery 'fur coat'. This dense pubescence is largely absent from frostweed, the most common wildflower to be mistaken for *Helianthemum dumosum*.

Likely places to search for bushy rockrose are areas which have been artificially kept open by human activity. The roughs of golf courses, (where native species have not been supplanted by turf grass

144

and ornamentals), powerline right-of-ways and the margins of airport runways create vestige habitats where the plant can flourish.

Bushy rockrose should be sought during its flowering period of late May to early June; it tends to become obscure among the tall grasses when in fruit. It seems ironic that this historic native of the Cape heathlands now depends on the clearing activities of Man, even while the 'natural' process of succession threatens its existence.

May-June   Sandplains; Dry Heaths

Bushy Rockrose   *Helianthemum dumosum*

Leafy White Orchid; Bog Candles   *Plantanthera dilatata*
                                       (Pursh)   Hook.

A first time sighting of the bog-candle in full flower leaves the beholder impressed by its beauty and size. Decorating a three to four foot high, leafy spike are dozens of snow white flowers. Their outstretched lateral sepals give the flowers a curious look resembling little Caspar the Friendly Ghosts or flying nuns. These odd blossoms are a delight from an olfactory aspect as well, exuding the spicy fragrance of cloves. This feature gives it the name 'scent bottle' in the northern Maritimes.

Bog candles is one of the largest of the so-called rein orchids. It is far more common in northern New England in the circumneutral, calcareous soils found there, than in the sandy, acidic soils of the Cape. Moist, spring-fed ditches and swales of the White Mountains is the habitat type one would normally associate with this impressive orchid.

There is but one colony of bog candles east of Worcester, a historic site in East Sandwich which has been watched closely by botanists for many years. The habitat is thick muck formed by spring seeps from a clay bank. There may be a buffering agent or calcium deposit, (perhaps from shells in an ancient Indian midden), to explain how this plant became established in so acidic and otherwise hostile an environment as Cape Cod.

This species is rare throughout the state, with only four recorded sites presently known in Massachusetts. It is listed as Threatened by the MNHP.

The numbers at the Sandwich colony have fluctuated, with seventeen robust plants recorded in 1988. This represents a high for the past five years and a 20% increase over the 1987 total. At one time it was thought bog candles were extirpated completely from Cape Cod. Any disturbance to the source of water for the springs in which it thrives will have dire consequences for our area's only population of this spectacular denizen of the North Country.

June-July   Spring Seeps

146

Leafy White Orchid; Bog Candles

Platanthera dilatata

Swamp Pink; Dragon Mouth   *Arethusa bulbosa*   L.

In Greek mythology, Diana, goddess of the woods, rewarded the water nymph Arethusa with everlasting beauty by transforming her to a cascading water fountain. Diana's bewitching powers live on to this day in the form of the elusive, exquisitely beautiful swamp pink.

If ever there existed a flower too lovely for its own good, it is the swamp pink. Arising as a leafless stem from a loosely-anchored bulb in late May, the single flower sports light pink to deep magenta petals and sepals surrounding a flowing (as in a water fountain?) bearded lip. This lip usually features three fringed lines of yellow or white, blueprinting the entrance route for the bumblebees which are its sole pollinators.

In an attempt to force its way to the nectary, the pollen mass is cemented to the bee's thorax, hopefully to be deposited at the next flower's stigma. With a successful seed-set of about 5%, this process works better on paper than in reality.

With only nine locations for this species left in the state, swamp pink is officially listed as Threatened by MNHP. Interestingly, most of these sites are in damp sphagnum or cranberry bogs along the coast. One especially healthy population exists in sphagnum moss just a few yards from a heavily travelled road in Wareham. This has led to speculation that the species needs at least some habitat disturbance to prevent succession from shading it out. Many inland sites have vanished beneath a woody canopy.

The loss of such an intricately-sculpted orchid from our region seems almost unavoidable. Never common, dragon mouth's habitat requirements, fertilization scheme and unusual beauty all work against it. Combine these problems with the omnipresent threat of development and it is not difficult to envision the day when the wonderful nymph of Diana no longer graces the bogs of the coastal plain.

June   Sphagnum Bogs

148

Swamp Pink; Dragon Mouth

Arethusa bulbosa

149

Golden Club   *Orontium aquaticum*   L.

An intriguing member of the Arum family, this aquatic perennial displays tiny greenish-yellow flowers crowded onto a golden, club-shaped spadix. Unlike its well-known brethren jack-in-the-pulpit and skunk cabbage, golden club has only a rudimentary sheath or spathe surrounding the spadix.

Found in the shallow waters of eutrophic ponds and sluggish streams, golden club's large, elliptic leaves seem to rise perfectly dry out of the water. This iridescent waterproofing once gave it the name "never-wet".

Golden club is primarily a coastal plain species, though there are two current inland sites in central Massachusetts. Reaching the very northern limit of its national range here in Barnstable County, nine of the state's eleven colonies are protected within the Cape Cod National Seashore in Provincetown. This is a salutary situation for the plant, as it is currently listed as threatened by the MNHP.

Rarity is a relative term in botany. While golden club is valued and protected in Massachusetts, it is reviled in the deep South as an aquatic nuisance and impediment to navigation. The Army Corps of Engineers is involved with programs to protect this plant in Monson, Massachusetts, while implementing plans to eradicate it down South.

Indians taught the colonists how to dry and powder the thick rootstock and seeds to make a nutritious flour. As with all members of the Arum family, merely boiling the roots will not remove the acrid, burning sensation of oxalic acid crystals found in these plants.

May-June   Shallow ponds

Golden Club *Orontium aquaticum*

151

Fringed Polygala   *Polygala paucifolia*   Willd.

Serendipity, the gift of finding something valuable accidentally, often plays a role in scientific discovery. So it was with Cape Cod's only record of fringed polygala.

This attractive wildflower was discovered growing in Bourne, in May of 1983, when a newly-carved subdivision road revealed the plant's hot pink blossoms to one of the authors while walking his dog. With the ever-present bulldozers poised to raze all native vegetation in the area, transplantation was necessary to save this remnant population.

With the assistance of the town Conservation Commission, the nine foot square colony was successfully moved to municipal conservation land where they are now flourishing.

Though a fairly common plant in central and western sections of New England, fringed polygala's only previous record in eastern Massachusetts was S.F. Blake's 1922 sighting in West Stoughton. The sandy, generally barren soil of the Cape makes this species' presence here a bit of a mystery, as it prefers the rich, humus-laden soils of western mainland sections.

The ornate flower structure of fringed polygala is typical of all members of the Milkwort family (*Polygalaceae*). The striking, rose-magenta flowers bear two lateral wings on either side of the fused petals , which form a sort of keel. This keel is crowned with a gaudy purple fringe of unknown function.The scientific name is from the Greek *polys gala* meaning 'much milk'. The Greek physician Dioscorides named it in the belief that ingestion of the plant increased milk production in dairy animals and even human mothers.

Its popularity among wildflower fanciers is attested to by its many colloquial names, including bird-on-the-wing, *gaywings*, flowering wintergreen and even baby-toes.

May   Rich Woods

152

Fringed Polygala   *Polygala paucifolia*

New England Thoroughwort

Eupatorium leucolepis
(DC.) Torr. & Gray
var. *novaeangliae* Fern.

New England thoroughwort's worldwide distribution is contained within two localities; Plymouth County in Massachusetts and Washington and Newport Counties in Rhode Island. Its hold on survival is slim to say the least, with its type station in Lakeville, where it was first discovered, reduced to a remnant two plants (Sorrie, 1986).

All Thoroughworts are a nondescript genus of plants, the most familiar being the abundant wetland plant, boneset (*Eupatorium perfoliatum*).While New England thoroughwort is a variety of a more common species found south of New England, its aspect is distinctive.

Stiffly erect with paired, sharply toothed leaves carried at an abrupt, ninety degree angle from the stem, this plant is quite unlike other Thoroughworts, though it does share the dingy-white corymb of undistinguished flowers characteristic of its fellow species. Its preferred habitat is the upper sandy margins of coastal plain kettle ponds, and therein lies the problem. Development and recreational pressures have created serious impacts on historical localities. A total of three historic sites have been lost to development in recent years; eight colonies still exist in the state, all in south Plymouth County.

With every 'pond view' house that goes up, the inevitable lure of the water produces private beaches, boat launches, docks and piers, all at a high cost to our native flora. Wise land stewardship by the landowner, tighter zoning or other regulatory controls on pondshore development, and a land acquisition program which targets delicate ecological areas like pondshores and wetlands are but three options to explore in protecting these rare kettle pond species.

The Nature Conservancy, in cooperation with the state Natural Heritage Program, has attempted to protect this emperiled plant through land acquisition of its habitat. A highway project was rerouted in Kingston to save a sizable colony. Thus it seems that despite its low profile and relatively unattractive appearance, New England thoroughwort's distinctive place as one of the few New England endemics has created a protective mechanism which one can only hope will be a success for it and other threatened plant species of our region.

August-Sept.   Gravel Shorelines of Ponds

New England Thoroughwort   *Eupatorium leucolepis*
var. *novaeangliae*

Plymouth Gentian   *Sabatia kennedyana*   Fern.

If there is one wildflower which symbolizes the fragile beauty of our many coastal plain kettle ponds, it is the incomparable Plymouth gentian.

An experience not soon forgotten is to walk the perimeter of a quiet pond in midsummer and be greeted there by a sea of pink garlanding the shoreline.

Even if the Plymouth gentian was not categorized by the Massachusetts Natural Heritage Program as a species of Special Concern, it would command a certain amount of attention and respect. Standing two to three feet tall, a single plant may bear up to twenty-four magenta to pink flowers. Each blossom contains nine to twelve petals, with a red-bordered yellow 'eye' in the center surrounding the pistil. A pure white form occurs in about one percent of the population.

While a feast for the eyes, Plymouth gentian is also an olfactory delight, emiting a delicate fragrance somewhat like lily-of-the-valley.

As with many plants which grow in the peaty margins of coastal kettle ponds, the Plymouth gentian's flowering emergence is dependent on how high pond levels are year to year.

In times of high water, *Sabatia* will flower along the upper apron above the water line. This gives the perennial rhizomes of submerged plants a dormancy period which helps to reinvigorate them. During periods of dry weather when water drawdown is maximized, literally thousands of Plymouth gentians may be seen ringing local kettle ponds.

While this species is certainly common to abundant within its southeastern Massachusetts stronghold, its status worldwide is another story. Of sixty-one sites left globally, forty-five are in the Bay State. The rest are scattered in Rhode Island, North and South Carolina and one disjunct population in the Tusket Valley, Yarmouth, Nova Scotia. Cape Codders are fortunate indeed, to boast of the world's most prolific populations of this famed wildflower.

Destruction of habitat by recreational vehicles, combined with an attractiveness which beckons 'pick me' to every passing walker, leaves this queen of the coastal plain vulnerable. Admire its beauty and fragrance, then go pick some daisies for the vase at home.

July-September   Wet Meadows; Pondshores

156

Plymouth Gentian   *Sabatia kennedyana*

Sandplain Gerardia
Agalinis acuta Penn.

Of all the wildflower species found in this publication, surely sandplain gerardia holds the least enviable title as the plant most likely to succumb to extinction. Once it flourished in the sandy heaths and 'downs' of the Cape and Islands. Now only two remnant enclaves remain in Nineteenth Century cemeteries in the upper Cape.

These two small colonies, along with three more discovered on Long Island and one recent sighting in Maryland, are all that's left of this diminutive member of the Figwort family. It is one of the very few New England species protected under the federal Endangered Species Act. This is exclusive company, as only three other New England plant species have attained Endangered or Threatened status under the ESA.

Like many plants adapted to the open, sandy moors once so integral a part of our region's landscape, the sandplain gerardia has been wiped out by natural succession to a pitch pine and oak overstory, a result of fire suppression and abandonment of agricultural and grazing practices. Wild grass fires and grazing kept the sandplains open, but fire and sheep are inimical to suburbanization. Historical sites on Martha's Vineyard and Nantucket, where many field researchers hold out hope of rediscovery, are now developed or shaded out.

The plant sports a pretty pink flower, resembling the funnel-shaped blossom of other common members familiar to many as the gerardias. Growing no more than six to eight inches high, this annual must set seed in order to propagate. That modern grazer called the mower could be the bane or blessing of this species; correct timing could keep competing vegetation out and help disperse viable seeds in the fall. In the past few years, however, mowing in the wrong place at the wrong time has probably impacted the two known cemetery populations.

When and if the tiny sandplain gerardia disappears from New England, perhaps only a few botanists will mourn its fate. Yet sadly, a direct link to Cap Cod's historic past, a past which itself is rapidly vanishing, will be gone forever.

August-October   Sand Plains; Heaths

158

Sandplain Gerardia   *Agalinis acuta*

Tinker's-weed; Wild Coffee   *Triosteum perfoliatum*   L.

As with fringed polygala, the discovery of the Commonwealth's first verified record of tinker's-weed in sixty-three years was a product of serendipity.

While on a proposed building site inspection for the Bourne Conservation Commission in 1985, the senior author discovered a coarse two foot high plant growing on a rocky wooded bank overlooking the Pocasset River.

The leaves were striking in appearance; wide, fiddle-shaped and completely fused around the stem, as if one leaf and not two. Nestled in the leaf axil against the stem were three to four orange fruit topped by the spidery sepals of the departed flowers. This dry drupe resembled an elongated rose hip in both texture and taste. Within were three stony-hard seeds.

This strange plant, one of only two herbaceous species found in the Honeysuckle family, was tinker's-weed, sometimes called wild coffee. Two years after its discovery, its current status is now being determined by the state Natural Heritage and Endangered Species Program, which is proposing it for Endangered classification.

Tinker's-weed has a long history in folk lore. Its deep taproot was used as an emetic for centuries, giving it two of its many English names, wood ipecac and fever root. The orange fruit was dried and ground into a fine substitute for coffee and is still used as such in the Appalachian Mountains, where it remains fairly common.

Current records show the Pocasset River site as the only existing colony left in the Commonwealth. No botanic sightings have been documented since 1925; there are only a total of eight historic records dating back to the 1800's.

Being at its very northern range limit in Massachusetts, it may never have been common here. As with many such herbs, its medicinal properties could have contributed to its own demise.

A fascinating corollary to the rediscovery of tinker's-weed is its possible value as an indicator of prehistoric archeological sites. This plant generally needs a richer, more alkaline soil than is found on acidic Cape Cod. Acting on the hunch that the plant's presence was due at least in part to unusual soil conditions, Fred Dunford, staff archeologist of the Cape Cod Musuem of Natural History conducted a limited dig in the area of the colony.

Just six inches down a sizable shell heap left by Cape Indians as long as one thousand years ago was discovered. These oyster, quahog and whelk shells (along with other artifacts and animal bones) provided a buffering agent (calcium) which created a higher soil PH, much to the liking of the *Triosteum.*Other uncommon Cape plant species such as wild columbine, agrimony and thimbleberry were also found on the site, further corroborating the theory that some plant species needing more neutral soils can act as indicators of Indian shell heaps or middens. This potential should not be lost on the scientific community.

In light of all this, town officials are negotiating with the landowner to spare the site from development. As this book goes to press, it appears these efforts may meet with success.It seems that some at least still give a tinker's-damn about tinker's-weed.

June-July   Rocky Woods

Tinker's-weed   *Triosteum perfoliatum*

Painted Trillium   *Trillium undulatum*

A Legacy of Flowers

How rapidly new flowers unfold! as if Nature would
get through her work too soon. One has as much as he
can do to observe how flowers successively unfold. It is
a flowery revolution, to which but few attend. Hardly
too much attention can be bestowed on flowers

— Henry D. Thoreau

On a recent botanic field trip in southeastern Massachusetts, my friend and I walked down one of those ubiquitous subdivision cul-de-sacs which rend our landscape everywhere these days. The sole silver lining to this cloud is that before any construction takes place, the bulldozer's cut actually opens up previously impenetrable woods, swamps and forests to the inquisitive botanist or naturalist.

As we climbed over a particularly large pile of excavated fill, we gazed down into the hemlock swamp which would soon be obliterated by house construction. To our delight and amazement, the soft knolls under the hemlocks were garlanded with dozens of painted trilliums (*Trillium undulatum*) in full bloom.

Never had I seen so much of this exquisite trillium, even in its more common habitat in western and northern New England. It was the first time I had found any trillium species in southeastern Massachusetts, where it is generally too sandy and nutrient-poor for this lover of rich soils. The thrill of discovering these lovely, native wildflowers was tempered by the thought of their imminent destruction. Did the developer or heavy-equipment operator know that their carefully

163

packaged and planned neighborhood project would wipe out one of the few remaining colonies of a plant clinging to existence here in eastern Massachusetts? More to the point, would they care?

Our region has seen a doubling of population since 1950. In the town of Brewster alone, year-round population has zoomed from 1,790 in 1970 to almost 8,000 in 1985. According to the 1987 Massachusetts Audubon report "Losing Ground", Cape Cod towns have been hit the hardest in the state by the rapacious development trend of the past five years. Four towns in particular, Mashpee, Brewster, Barnstable and Sandwich, lost over 7,000 acres of land to development since 1981.

The stress this kind of habitat destruction has on our native plants and animals is enormous. Many species, once part of our natural legacy, are either gone or survive in small enclaves provided by parklands, utility line right of ways, old cemeteries and public and private land trusts.

Is the saving of trilliums more important than the discovery of a cure for cancer? Certainly not. Yet a small, seemingly insignificant pink flower of the Vinca genus found in Madagascar has cut fatalities from childhood leukemia almost in half. Will future scientific studies reveal an important medical use for the painted trillium?

Even if a beautiful wildflower fails to provide us with some material comfort such as medicine, food or clothing, every species is an integral cog in a most important mechanism, natural diversity. For each species lost to development, another dozen dependent species are also threatened. The delicate linkage among all living things begins to breakdown as natural diversity shrinks in the wake of unplanned or uncaring development.

Aside from the practical arguments for wildflower preservation, one which should not be overlooked is the joy of discovering the year's first blossoming of trailing arbutus, pink ladies-slippers or Plymouth gentian. These gifts of color, form and fragrance come to us each year with a regularity and dependence rare in our lives.

With no fancy fertilizers, phosphates or pesticides, wild-flowers lend a dimension to our world both free and priceless. As Emerson once wrote,

Beauty is its own excuse for being.

— mjd

164

State-listed Rare Flowers
Cape Cod and South Plymouth County

Barnstable County ranks fifth in total number of state listed rare plants (MNHP, 1985). There are 52 rare list species for Cape Cod out of 242 designated statewide. The following is a listing of what most people would call wildflowers, which excludes grasses, sedges, rushes and ferns. Rarity classifications include: *Endangered*; any species documented to be in danger of extirpation from the state; *Threatened*; a species documented to be likely of extirpation if recent declines go unchecked; *Special Concern* indicates a species of such small numbers or limited distribution that it could become threatened in the near future, and *Watch List*, species which, while not actually rare, live in habitat threatened by development and have had documented declines in recent years.

Species	Classification	Habitat
Naiad *Najas guadalupensis*	Watch List	Salt Ponds
Terete Arrowhead *Sagittaria teres*	Special Concern	Freshwater Ponds
Golden Club *Orontium aquaticum*	Threatened	Shallow Ponds
Redroot *Lachnanthes caroliana*	Special Concern	Peaty Pondshores
Sand Plain Blue-eyed Grass *Sisyrinchium fuscatum*	Special Concern	Dry Heaths

Arethusa *Arethusa bulbosa*	Threatened	Sphagnum Bogs
Large Whorled Pogonia *Isotria verticillata*	Watch List	Rich Woods
Heartleaf Twayblade *Listera cordata*	Endangered	White Cedar Swamps
Leafy White Orchid *Platanthera dilatata*	Threatened	Limey Spring Seeps
Little Ladies'-tresses *Spiranthes tuberosa*	Watch List	Sandplains
Spring Ladies'-tresses *Spiranthes vernalis*	Special Concern	Fields; Meadows
Cranefly Orchid *Tipularia discolor*	Endangered	Oak-Holly Forests
Pondshore Knotweed *Polygonum puritanorum*	Special Concern	Freshwater Ponds
Strigose Knotweed *Polygonum setaceum* var. interjectum	Special Concern	Rich Streamsides
Matted Sea-Blite *Sueda americana*	Special Concern	Salt Mudflats
Narrow-leaved Spring Beauty *Claytonia virginica*	Threatened	Rich Thickets
Thread-leaved Sundew *Drosera filiformis*	Watch List	Sandy Pondshores
Sandplain Flax *Linum intercursum*	Special Concern	Dry Open Fields
Nuttall's Milkwort *Polygala nuttalii*	Watch List	Dry Open Sand
Broom Crowberry *Corema conradii*	Special Concern	Heaths and Barrens
Creeping St. John's-wort *Hypericum adpressum*	Threatened	Fresh Pondshores
Bushy Rockrose *Helianthemum dumosum*	Special Concern	Dry Open Fields
Prickly Pear Cactus *Opuntia humifusa*	Threatened	Dry Sterile Fields

Maryland Meadow-beauty *Rhexia mariana*	Endangered	Peaty Pondshores
Slender Marsh Pink *Sabatia campanulata*	Endangered	Peaty Pondshores
Plymouth Gentian *Sabatia kennedyana*	Special Concern	Fresh Pondshores
Butterfly-weed *Asclepias tuberosa*	Watch List	Dry Fields
Oysterleaf *Mertensia maritima*	Endangered	Rocky Shorelines
Hyssop Hedge-nettle *Stachys hyssopifolia*	Watch List	Dry or Wet Fields
Sandplain Gerardia *Agalinis acuta*	Endangered	Dry Sandplains
Two Flowered Bladderwort *Utricularia biflora*	Threatened	Muddy Pondshores
Fibrous Bladderwort *Utricularia fibrosa*	Threatened	Rich Pondshores
Subulate Bladderwort *Utricularia subulata*	Special Concern	Sphagnum Bogs
Tinker's Weed *Triosteum perfoliatum*	Endangered	Rocky Woods
New England Boneset *Eupatorium leucolepis* var. *novaeangliae*	Endangered	Peaty Pondshores
New England Blazing-star Liatris scariosa var. *novaeangliae*	Special Concern	Sandplain Grasslands
Seabeach Dock *Rumex pallidus*	Threatened	Rocky Beaches
Whorled Milkwort *Polygala verticillata*	Watch List	Sandplain Grasslands
Purple Milkweed *Asclepias purpurascens*	Threatened	Thin Woods
Nantucket Shadbush *Amelanchier nantucketensis*	Special Concern	Heaths; Grasslands

Index

The Library of Congress has cataloged the original edition as follows:

DiGregorio, Mario.
    A vanishing heritage: wildflowers of Cape Cod / Mario DiGregorio
and Jeff Wallner.
        p.   cm.
    Includes index.
    ISBN 0–87842–231–5
    1. Wild flowers—Massachusetts—Cape Cod—Identification.
2. Wild flowers—Massachusetts—Cape Cod—Pictorial works.
3. Rare plants—Massachusetts—Cape Cod—Identification. 4. Rare
plants—Massachusetts—Cape Cod—Pictorial works. I. Title
QK166.D53 1989   89–30718
582.13'09744'92—dc19   CIP